Sunset

Gifts from Your Kitchen

BY THE EDITORS OF SUNSET BOOKS
AND SUNSET MAGAZINE

Lane Publishing Co. • Menlo Park, California

Research & Text

**Mary Jane Swanson
Cynthia Overbeck Bix**

Coordinating Editor

Deborah Thomas Kramer

Design

Cynthia Hanson

Illustrations

Dick Cole

Photography

Tom Wyatt

Photo Stylist

JoAnn Masaoka

Cover: Some examples of special food gifts are aromatic Tarragon Vinegar (page 86), Apricot Jam (page 62), Party Bread Sticks (page 22), Thumbprint Cookies (page 48), and Coconut Butter Cookies (page 49). Cover design by Sandra Popovich. Photo styling by JoAnn Masaoka. Food styling by Judith A. Gaulke. Photography by Tom Wyatt.

ABOUT THE RECIPES

All of the recipes in this book were tested and developed in the *Sunset* test kitchens.

Home Economics Editor,
Sunset Magazine
Jerry Anne DiVecchio

Whimsical piglets recline atop gift terrines of rich, elegantly garnished Glazed Chicken Liver Pâté. For the recipe, turn to page 8.

GIFTS FROM THE HEART...

A gift of food that you make in your own kitchen is one of the most thoughtful ways to say thank you, happy holidays, welcome home... or simply to express your love and friendship at any time. And good food is something that pleases everybody.

Food gifts can be simple or elaborate, carefully planned or spur-of-the-moment. You may want to plan ahead and bake a dozen little loaves of bread and make a dozen jars of jam to pair as gifts at holiday time. Or you may decide to whip up a batch of hot seasoned popcorn just before you set out with a friend to watch a football game. Perhaps you'll want to carefully shape some delicious homemade candies, or maybe you prefer simply to add a few sprigs of fresh herbs to flavor a bottle of special vinegar for giving.

Whatever your inclinations and time, you're sure to find just the right recipe in this book. Beginning with appetizers and snacks, our selection runs the gamut from quick and yeast breads to cakes, cookies, and candies to sweet and savory preserves. We even give you instructions for creating elaborate theme gift baskets for very special occasions. All of our recipes include information on preparation and storage times to help you choose the most appropriate recipe for your needs.

In addition, we provide helpful tips on mailing your gifts, as well as a wealth of ideas and instructions for packaging them... from stenciling or stamping your own gift tags to creating original packages for cookies, candies, or other foods. From the outside in, your gifts of food are certain to be original, appealing, and deeply appreciated.

For their valuable assistance in helping to prepare this book, we'd like to thank Joan Griffiths and Sandra Popovich. Special thanks go to Rebecca LaBrum for her skillful and creative editing of the manuscript. We're also grateful to the Cotton Works, Crate & Barrel, and Keeping Traditions for their generosity in sharing props for use in our photographs.

Sunset Books
  Editor: David E. Clark
  Managing Editor: Elizabeth L. Hogan

First printing May 1988

CONTENTS

SPECIAL FEATURES

♥ ♥ ♥

APPETIZERS & SNACKS

Out-of-the-ordinary gifts that can't miss

Whether you're looking for an hors d'oeuvre to contribute to a dinner party or a distinctive food gift for a friend, one of the irresistible appetizers or snacks in this chapter is sure to fit the bill of fare. If elegance is what you're after, choose small nut-studded cheeses, a picture-pretty aspic-glazed Brie, creamy chicken liver pâté, or a layered cheese torta— all go together easily despite their impressive appearance. You might present them on a small cutting board or in a basket lined with green leaves, along with a fresh baguette or crackers and perhaps a fancy little hors d'oeuvres knife.

We also offer an appealing selection of butter-rich cheese pastries, spiced nuts, and seasoned popcorn. All are good as appetizers or snacks, and they look attractive packaged in glass jars or canisters, in tins or baskets, or on handsome trays or plates. Note that some of the gifts in this chapter require refrigeration; for these, be sure to add a tag or card giving storing and serving instructions.

Chèvre in Olive Oil

♥ ♥ ♥

Preparation time: 10 minutes, plus at least 1 week to marinate
Storage time: Up to 1 month at room temperature

The gourmets among your friends will appreciate a pretty jar of chèvre in olive oil seasoned with chiles and herbs. Suggest serving the marinated cheese with toasted rounds of French bread.

About 1½ cups olive oil
¾ **pound log-shaped soft unripened chèvre (plain or with any coating trimmed off), cut into 1-inch-thick slices**
6 **sprigs dry thyme, *each* about 3 inches long, or 1 tablespoon dry thyme leaves**
2 **sprigs dry rosemary, *each* about 3 inches long, or 2 teaspoons dry rosemary**
2 **teaspoons whole black peppercorns**
2 **small dried hot red chiles**
1 **or 2 cloves garlic**

Pour 1½ cups of the oil into one 3-cup jar or two 1½-cup jars. Add chèvre, thyme, rosemary, peppercorns, chiles, and garlic (if using 2 jars, add 1 small clove garlic to each). If necessary, add more oil to cover cheese. Cover jars tightly. Before giving, let stand at room temperature for at least 1 week (cheese will keep for up to 1 month). Makes 1 large or 2 small jars of appetizer cheese.

Stuffed Gouda Cheese

♥ ♥ ♥

Preparation time: 20 to 30 minutes
Storage time: Up to 1 week in refrigerator

Turn a whole Gouda cheese into something special when you use its red-waxed rind as a container for a hearty, beer-flavored spread. Include a loaf of pumpernickel with the cheese, if you like.

1 **whole baby Gouda cheese (about 14 oz.)**
½ **cup beer**
1 **teaspoon Dijon mustard**
⅛ **teaspoon ground nutmeg**
¼ **cup butter or margarine, cut into chunks, at room temperature**
½ **teaspoon caraway seeds**

Cut out a circle from center top of cheese. Carefully scoop out cheese inside, leaving shell intact. Use a curved small knife, such as a grapefruit knife, to remove cheese at first; finish the job with a small spoon, scooping carefully to avoid puncturing shell. Cut any large pieces of cheese into cubes.

Place ¼ cup of the beer in a food processor or blender. Add cheese, mustard, nutmeg, and butter. Whirl until smooth, gradually adding remaining ¼ cup beer with motor running. Stir in caraway seeds. Spoon cheese mixture into shell. (Not all of the mixture will fit; reserve extra for other uses.) Wrap airtight; store in refrigerator for up to 1 week. On gift tag, note that cheese should be served at room temperature. Makes 1 large appetizer cheese (about 1½ cups spread).

Nut-coated Garlic-Herb Cheese

Preparation time: 20 to 30 minutes, plus 1 hour to chill
Storage time: Up to 3 days in refrigerator

Flavored with garlic, savory, and black pepper, these little cheeses are reminiscent of French Boursin. For giving, cover them with a "gift wrap" of toasted nuts.

⅔ **to ¾ cup pine nuts**
1 **large package (8 oz.) cream cheese, at room temperature**
3 **tablespoons lemon juice**
½ **teaspoon dry or 1 teaspoon minced fresh winter or summer savory leaves**
¼ **to ½ teaspoon freshly ground black pepper**
1 **clove garlic, minced or pressed**
Whipping cream or milk

Spread pine nuts in a shallow baking pan. Toast in a 350° oven until golden brown (8 to 12 minutes), shaking pan frequently. Set aside.

In small bowl of an electric mixer, beat cream cheese until smooth. Beat in lemon juice, savory, pepper, and garlic. If mixture is too thick, beat in a little cream.

To shape, divide cheese mixture in half. Spoon each half onto a piece of plastic wrap at least 15 inches long. Wrap tightly, pushing out any air bubbles. Pinch and shape wrapped cheese into a flat round, triangle, or square. Refrigerate until firm (at least 1 hour).

Unwrap cheese and set on a gift board or plate; then press toasted pine nuts into cheese in a neat pattern, covering entire surface. Wrap airtight; store in refrigerator for up to 3 days. Makes 2 appetizer cheese rounds.

Layered Cheese Tortas

(Pictured on facing page)

♥ ♥ ♥

Preparation time: About 45 minutes, plus about 1 hour to chill
Storage time: Up to 5 days in refrigerator

Italian in origin, these colorful striped tortas make a dramatic appetizer. To prepare them, you simply layer a buttery cheese mixture with your choice of three fillings in a mold.

On your gift tag, suggest serving the tortas with sliced baguettes or crudités.

>   Topping & filling (choices and recipes follow)
> 2 large packages (8 oz. *each*) cream cheese, at room temperature
> 2 cups (1 lb.) unsalted butter, at room temperature

Prepare topping and filling of your choice; set aside. In large bowl of an electric mixer, beat cream cheese and butter until very smoothly blended, stopping to scrape down bowl sides as needed.

Smoothly line a 5- to 6-cup plain mold, such as a loaf pan or clean flowerpot, with a double layer of moistened cheesecloth. (Or use two 2½- to 3-cup molds.) Drape excess cloth over rim of mold.

Set topping in mold bottom. With your fingers or a rubber spatula, spread a thin layer of cheese mixture over topping. Cover with a thin layer of filling, extending it evenly to sides of mold. Repeat layers until mold is filled, ending with cheese. (If using 2 molds, use half the cheese mixture and half the filling in each.)

Fold ends of cheesecloth over torta and press down lightly to compact. Fold back cloth; invert torta onto a serving dish and gently pull off cloth. Refrigerate until firm (about 1 hour), then wrap airtight and store in refrigerator for up to 5 days. Makes 1 large torta or 2 smaller tortas.

Pesto Topping & Filling. Put a **fresh basil sprig** (brushed with **salad oil**) in bottom of each mold for topping. For filling, in a food processor or blender, whirl to a paste 3¼ cups lightly packed **fresh basil leaves,** 1½ cups (about 7½ oz.) freshly grated **Parmesan or Romano cheese,** and ½ cup **olive oil.** Stir in 6 tablespoons **pine nuts** and season to taste with **salt** and **pepper.**

Ripe Olive Topping & Filling. Put 2 to 4 **pitted ripe olives** in bottom of each mold for topping.

For filling, spoon off and discard excess oil from top of 1 jar or can (6 to 7 oz.) **tapenade** (ripe olive purée). Combine purée with ½ cup **pine nuts.**

Sun-dried Tomato Topping & Filling. Drain 1 jar (10½ oz.) **sun-dried tomatoes in olive oil,** reserving 2 tablespoons of the oil. For topping, split 1 tomato in half; arrange in mold bottom. (If using 2 molds, use ½ tomato in each mold.)

For filling, whirl remaining tomatoes with reserved oil in a blender or food processor until finely chopped.

Aspic-glazed Brie

♥ ♥ ♥

Preparation time: About 1 hour, plus 1 hour to chill coated cheese
Storage time: Up to 3 days in refrigerator

Dressed up with fresh flowers or herbs and a shimmering aspic glaze, wedges or wheels of Brie cheese make especially handsome gifts.

> 2 cups dry white wine
> 1 envelope unflavored gelatin
> 4 small wheels or wedges (3 oz. *each*) or 2 large wheels or wedges (about 9 oz. *each*) Brie cheese, chilled
>   Decorations (suggestions follow)

In a 2- to 3-quart pan, combine wine and gelatin; let stand for 5 minutes. Place over medium heat; stir until gelatin dissolves and mixture is clear.

Place pan in a larger container filled with ice water. Stir liquid occasionally until it begins to thicken and look syrupy; stir slowly to prevent bubbles from forming. If aspic becomes too firm, reheat to soften, then chill again until syrupy.

Set cold cheese on a rack in a shallow rimmed pan. Spoon a coat of aspic over top and sides of cheese; when aspic is slightly tacky (1 to 3 minutes), arrange decorations atop cheese in desired pattern. Refrigerate entire pan with rack and cheese, uncovered, for about 15 minutes.

Carefully spoon more aspic over top and sides of cheese; refrigerate until tacky. If necessary, add 1 or 2 more coats, refrigerating after each layer is added, in order to cover all exposed portions of decoration. When cheese is completely covered with aspic, invert a bowl over cheese without touching surface and refrigerate until firm (at least 1 hour) or for up to 3 days. Makes 4 small or 2 large wheels or wedges of decorated cheese.

Decorations. Use **fresh herbs** such as chives, dill, sage, thyme, tarragon, or cilantro (coriander), or **flowers** (or petals) such as pansies, roses, primroses, nasturtiums, violets, or strawberry blossoms.

To prepare, rinse gently, blot with paper towels, and refrigerate until ready to use (up to 1 day).

Colorful stripes of sun-dried tomato, pesto, or ripe olive
filling give these Layered Cheese Tortas (recipe on facing page) a festive look. To present
the rich-tasting appetizers as gifts, set them on a board
or wicker tray lined with shiny aralia leaves, then cover with plastic wrap or
cellophane. Tie the "package" with a ribbon.

PORK RILLETTES

♥ ♥ ♥

Preparation time: 45 to 60 minutes, plus about 4 hours to bake meat
Storage time: Up to 3 days in refrigerator; up to 1 month in freezer

French in origin, this wonderfully hearty spread (pronounce it ree-YET) for baguettes or crudités makes a delightful addition to a picnic hamper or to an appetizer buffet. Present it in small crocks or terrines.

    3 pounds boneless pork (shoulder or
       butt), cut into 1½-inch cubes
    1 teaspoon *each* salt and pepper
    1 clove garlic, minced or pressed
    ½ teaspoon dry thyme leaves
    1 bay leaf
    ½ cup *each* dry white wine and water
    ½ cup (¼ lb.) unsalted butter or margarine,
       at room temperature
       Chopped parsley

Place pork in a 4- to 5-quart casserole or pan with heatproof handles; add salt, pepper, garlic, thyme, bay leaf, wine, and water. Cover tightly and bake in a 250° oven until meat falls apart in shreds when prodded with a fork (about 4 hours).

Discard bay leaf. Drain meat, reserving juices. Let meat cool, then shred it with your fingers or 2 forks. Let juices cool; skim and discard fat. With a heavy spoon or your hands, combine meat, juices, and butter until well blended. Add more salt, if desired. Spoon into five 1-cup crocks or terrines. Cover airtight; store in refrigerator for up to 3 days, in freezer for up to 1 month. Before giving, sprinkle with parsley. On gift tag, note that rillettes should be served at room temperature. Makes 5 (1-cup) crocks or terrines of rillettes.

♥ CHICKEN OR TURKEY RILLETTES

Follow directions for **Pork Rillettes,** but instead of pork, use about 3½ pounds **chicken or turkey legs** with thighs attached. Cut legs apart if necessary to make them fit pan easily. Also add ½ teaspoon **dry rosemary** and ¼ cup finely chopped **shallots** or green onions (including tops); reduce wine and water to ⅓ cup *each*. Bake as directed. When you shred meat, discard skin, bones, and tendons; finely chop shredded meat with a knife. Makes 5 (1-cup) crocks or terrines of rillettes.

♥ RABBIT RILLETTES

Follow directions for **Pork Rillettes,** but use 1 **rabbit** (2½ to 3 lbs.), cut up, instead of pork. Also add ½ teaspoon **dry rosemary** and ¼ cup finely chopped **shallots** or green onions (including tops); reduce wine and water to ⅓ cup *each*. Bake as directed. When you shred meat, discard bones. Makes 4 (1-cup) crocks or terrines of rillettes.

GLAZED CHICKEN LIVER PÂTÉ

(Pictured on page 2)

Preparation time: 35 to 45 minutes, plus 2 hours to chill and glaze
Storage time: Up to 2 days in refrigerator

For a delightful double gift, present this creamy pâté, glazed and decorated, in a ceramic terrine or stoneware crock.

    1½ pounds chicken livers
    1½ cups (¾ lb.) butter or margarine
     6 tablespoons chopped onion
     2 teaspoons dry mustard
     ½ teaspoon *each* salt, ground nutmeg, and
        anchovy paste
     ¼ teaspoon *each* ground red pepper
        (cayenne) and ground cloves
        Chives and carrot slices
    1½ teaspoons unflavored gelatin
     ½ cup water
     ½ cup condensed consommé

Place livers in a 3- to 4-quart pan and cover with water; bring to a boil. Reduce heat, cover, and simmer until livers are just firm (12 to 15 minutes). Let cool in liquid for 15 minutes.

Drain livers and whirl in a food processor or blender until smooth. Add butter and whirl until fluffy. Add onion, mustard, salt, nutmeg, anchovy paste, red pepper, and cloves; whirl until well blended. Spread mixture evenly in two 2½- to 3-cup or four 1¼- to 1½-cup terrines or crocks. Press lightly to smooth surface. Arrange chives and carrot slices on pâté; press lightly to imbed in pâté. Cover and refrigerate until firm (at least 1 hour).

In a small pan, combine gelatin and water; let stand for 5 minutes. Add consommé and heat, stirring occasionally, until gelatin dissolves. Let cool to room temperature; spoon evenly over pâté. Refrigerate until gelatin is set (at least 1 hour) or for up to 2 days. Makes 2 (about 3-cup) or 4 (about 1½-cup) terrines or crocks of pâté.

CHEESE-HERB PRETZELS

not great for effort

(Pictured on page 10)

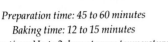

Preparation time: 45 to 60 minutes
Baking time: 12 to 15 minutes
Storage time: Up to 2 days at room temperature;
up to 1 month in freezer

Light and flaky, these tasty pastries are good as appetizers or accompaniments for soup or salad. Choose herb-seasoned pretzels or seed-coated, ginger-spiced twists—or make some of each.

>   1   cup all-purpose flour
>   2   tablespoons grated Parmesan cheese
>   ½   teaspoon garlic powder
>   ¼   teaspoon *each* dry basil, dry rosemary, and dry oregano leaves
>   ½   cup (¼ lb.) firm butter or margarine
>   1   cup (4 oz.) shredded sharp Cheddar cheese
>   2 to 3 tablespoons cold water

In a large bowl, stir together flour, Parmesan cheese, garlic powder, basil, rosemary, and oregano. Using a pastry blender or 2 knives, cut in butter until mixture resembles fine crumbs. Stir in Cheddar cheese.

Sprinkle water over flour mixture, 1 tablespoon at a time, stirring lightly with a fork until dough holds together. Gather dough into a ball with your hands. Divide dough in half, then cut each half into 12 equal pieces. (If dough is soft, wrap in plastic wrap and refrigerate until firm.)

Place each piece of dough on a lightly floured board; roll with your palms to make an 11-inch strand. Twist each strand into a pretzel shape. Place pretzels slightly apart on ungreased baking sheets. Bake in a 425° oven until golden brown (12 to 15 minutes). Transfer to racks; let cool completely.

Wrap airtight; store at room temperature for up to 2 days, in freezer for up to 1 month. Recrisp frozen pastries before giving: arrange (still frozen) on baking sheets and bake in a 350° oven until hot (5 to 7 minutes). Makes 2 dozen pastries.

♥ CHEESE TWISTS

(Pictured on page 10)

To prepare dough, stir together 1 cup **all-purpose flour** and ½ teaspoon *each* **salt** and **ground ginger** in a large bowl. Using a pastry blender or 2 knives, cut in ⅓ cup firm **butter** or margarine until mixture resembles fine crumbs. Stir in 1 cup (4 oz.) shredded **sharp Cheddar cheese.**

Blend 2 to 3 tablespoons **cold water** with ½ teaspoon **Worcestershire;** sprinkle over flour mixture, 1 tablespoon at a time, stirring lightly with a fork until dough holds together. Gather into a ball.

On a lightly floured board, roll dough out to a 10-inch square. Lightly beat 1 **egg;** brush over dough. Sprinkle dough evenly with 2 tablespoons **sesame, caraway, or poppy seeds** or coarse (kosher-style) salt. Cut dough square in half; cut each half into ½-inch-wide, 5-inch-long strips. Hold each strip at both ends and twist in opposite directions.

Place twists 1 inch apart on greased baking sheets. Bake in a 400° oven until golden brown (10 to 12 minutes). Let cool, wrap, store, and recrisp as directed for **Cheese-Herb Pretzels.** Makes 40 pastries.

CHEESE SPRITZ

(Pictured on page 10)

Preparation time: About 45 minutes
Baking time: 10 to 12 minutes
Storage time: Up to 2 days at room temperature;
up to 1 month in freezer

Shape these melt-in-the-mouth pastries with a cookie press, using a star or other decorative plate.

>   ⅔   cup butter or margarine, at room temperature
>   ½   cup shredded sharp Cheddar cheese
>   1   egg
>   ⅛   teaspoon ground red pepper (cayenne)
>   ¼   teaspoon dry mustard
>   ½   teaspoon *each* salt and sugar
>   1⅔ cups all-purpose flour
>   Poppy or sesame seeds

In large bowl of an electric mixer, beat together butter and cheese. Add egg, red pepper, mustard, salt, and sugar; beat until well blended. Gradually add flour, stirring until smoothly blended. Shape dough into a ball with your hands.

Firmly pack dough into a cookie press fitted with a decorative plate. Shape pastries on ungreased baking sheets, spacing them about 1 inch apart. Sprinkle with poppy seeds. Bake in a 375° oven until lightly browned (10 to 12 minutes). Transfer to racks and let cool completely. Wrap airtight; store at room temperature for up to 2 days, in freezer for up to 1 month. Recrisp frozen pastries before giving following directions for Cheese-Herb Pretzels (at left). Makes about 2½ dozen pastries.

Crunchy nuts, seasoned popcorn, or melt-in-your-mouth
cheese pastries are welcome gifts for any hostess. Packaged for giving here are
Chili Peanuts, Savory Almonds, Penuche Pecans,
and Curried Cashews & Raisins (all on facing page) in apothecary jars; spicy
Seasoned Popcorn (facing page) in a hand-stenciled basket;
and three kinds of cheese pastries (page 9) on a wooden tray.

SEASONED NUTS

(Pictured on facing page)

Preparation time: 20 to 30 minutes
Storage time: Up to 1 week at room temperature

Quick and easy to make, seasoned nuts appeal to just about everyone. Here, we suggest snappy chili-spiced peanuts, almonds with your choice of four coatings, curried cashews mixed with raisins, and—for the sweet tooth—brown sugar–coated Penuche Pecans.

♥ CHILI PEANUTS

Spread 2 cups (about 11 oz.) **raw Spanish peanuts** in a rimmed 10- by 15-inch baking pan. Bake in a 350° oven, stirring occasionally, until nuts are pale golden beneath skins (about 15 minutes). Remove from oven and sprinkle with 2 teaspoons **chili powder,** 1 teaspoon **ground cumin,** ½ to ¾ teaspoon **crushed red pepper,** and 1 tablespoon **salad oil.** Mix well. Return to oven; continue to bake, stirring once, until nuts are golden brown (8 to 10 more minutes). Sprinkle with **salt** to taste. Let cool completely. Package airtight; store at room temperature for up to 1 week. Makes 2 cups.

♥ SAVORY ALMONDS

Generously grease a rimmed 10- by 15-inch baking pan with 2 tablespoons **butter** or margarine; set aside. In a medium-size bowl, beat 1 **egg white** until frothy. Stir in 3 cups (1 lb.) **whole blanched almonds;** then mix in 1 tablespoon **coarse (kosher-style) salt,** seasoned salt, or Mexican seasoning or 2 tablespoons grated Parmesan cheese.

Spread nuts in baking pan; bake in a 325° oven until shiny and golden brown (about 20 minutes), stirring occasionally. Remove from pan while still warm. Let cool completely. Package airtight; store at room temperature for up to 1 week. Makes 3 cups.

♥ CURRIED CASHEWS & RAISINS

Spread 1½ cups (about 9 oz.) **raw cashews** in a rimmed 10- by 15-inch baking pan. Bake in a 350° oven, stirring occasionally, until pale golden (about 15 minutes). Remove from oven and sprinkle with 1 teaspoon *each* **ground coriander** and **ground**

cumin; ¼ teaspoon **ground turmeric;** ⅛ teaspoon *each* **ground red pepper** (cayenne) and **ground cloves;** ½ cup **raisins;** and 1 tablespoon **salad oil.** Mix well. Return to oven and continue to bake, stirring once, until cashews are golden (8 to 10 more minutes). Sprinkle with **salt** to taste. Let cool completely. Package airtight; store at room temperature for up to 1 week. Makes 2 cups.

♥ PENUCHE PECANS

In a 2-quart pan, combine 1 cup firmly packed **brown sugar,** ¼ teaspoon *each* **salt** and **ground cinnamon,** and 6 tablespoons **milk;** stir to blend. Cook over medium heat, stirring occasionally, until mixture reaches 236°F (soft ball stage) on a candy thermometer. Remove from heat and stir in 1 teaspoon *each* **vanilla** and grated **orange peel** and 3 cups (1½ lbs.) **pecan or walnut halves.** Continue to stir until mixture begins to lose its gloss and a sugary coating forms on nuts.

Turn mixture onto parchment paper. Using 2 forks, separate nuts. Let cool completely. Package airtight; store at room temperature for up to 1 week. Makes 3 cups.

SEASONED POPCORN

(Pictured on facing page)

Preparation time: 10 to 15 minutes, including time to pop corn
Storage time: Up to 1 day (or less, for best flavor)

Everybody likes popcorn! Perked up with a special seasoning, it's a gift that can't miss. For best flavor, give the same day you make it.

- ¼ cup butter or margarine, melted
- 1 clove garlic, minced or pressed
- ¾ teaspoon chili powder
- ½ teaspoon onion salt
- ¼ teaspoon crushed red pepper
- 15 cups hot popped popcorn (about ¾ cup unpopped)

Combine butter, garlic, chili powder, onion salt, and red pepper; pour over hot popcorn. Toss to blend. Let cool completely, package airtight, and store at room temperature for up to 1 day.

On gift tag, suggest reheating popcorn before serving: spread popcorn in an even, single layer in rimmed baking pans. Bake in a 350° oven until hot and crisp (5 to 8 minutes). Makes 15 cups.

QUICK BREADS

Easy to make, a delight to receive

Whether they take the form of tempting loaves, luscious coffee cakes, or dainty muffins or scones, quick breads make a distinctive gift for any taste or occasion. Warm up the crisp days of autumn with spicy, fragrant pumpkin or cranberry loaves. Say "Merry Christmas" with rich fruit-studded offerings. Celebrate spring with special sweet breads or muffins, or give a pan of savory cornbread or streusel-topped fresh fruit coffee cake any time.

As the name implies, quick breads go together quickly, and they're likewise easy to package and transport. Loaves can be baked, wrapped, and decorated right in give-away foil pans; just let them cool, then wrap in cellophane or plastic wrap and tie with a ribbon. Muffins and scones lend themselves to presentation in all kinds of pretty baskets and tins. These smaller breads taste best served soft and warm, so plan to give them on the day you bake them—or add a gift tag with reheating instructions. No matter what kind of quick bread you choose to bake, you'll find it a gift that's easy to make, fun to wrap, and delicious to receive.

IRISH SODA BREAD

♥ ♥ ♥

Preparation time: About 25 minutes
Baking time: 30 to 35 minutes
Storage time: Up to 1 day at room temperature; up to 1 month in freezer

This classic all-occasion recipe is so quick and easy to make, you'll surely want to bake multiple batches. A jar of jam or marmalade makes a welcome accompaniment to the round, fragrant loaves.

- 4 **cups all-purpose flour**
- 1 **teaspoon** *each* **salt and baking soda**
- 1 **tablespoon baking powder**
- ¼ **cup sugar (optional)**
- ⅛ **teaspoon ground cardamom or coriander (optional)**
- ¼ **cup firm butter or margarine**
- 1 **egg**
- 1¾ **cups buttermilk**

In a large bowl, stir together the flour, salt, baking soda, baking powder, sugar (if used), and cardamom (if used). Cut in butter with a pastry blender or 2 knives until mixture is crumbly. In another bowl, lightly beat egg and mix with buttermilk; stir into dry ingredients until blended. Turn dough out onto a floured board and knead until smooth (2 to 3 minutes).

Divide dough in half and shape each half into a smooth, round loaf; place each loaf in a greased 8-inch cake or pie pan and press to make dough fill pans. With a razor blade or floured sharp knife, cut a ½-inch-deep cross in top of each loaf.

Bake in a 375° oven until nicely browned (30 to 35 minutes). Turn loaves out of pans onto racks and let cool completely. Wrap airtight; store at room temperature for up to 1 day, in freezer for up to 1 month (thaw frozen bread wrapped). On gift tag, suggest reheating bread before serving: place on a baking sheet, cover loosely with foil, and heat in a 350° oven until hot (15 to 20 minutes). Makes 2 loaves.

♥ CURRANT SODA BREAD

Follow directions for **Irish Soda Bread;** use sugar but omit cardamom or coriander. After cutting in butter, add 2 cups **currants** or raisins and, if desired, 1¼ teaspoons **caraway seeds.**

♥ WHOLE WHEAT SODA BREAD

Follow directions for **Irish Soda Bread,** but substitute 2 cups **whole wheat flour** for 2 cups of the all-purpose flour. After cutting in butter, add 1 to 2 cups **raisins** or snipped pitted dates, if desired.

MEXICANA CORNBREAD

(Pictured on page 23)

Preparation time: 15 to 20 minutes
Baking time: About 35 minutes for 8-inch square pan; 15 to 20 minutes for small breads
Storage time: Up to 1 day at room temperature; up to 1 month in freezer (do not freeze bread made with avocado)

To give this pepper-laced cornbread a south-of-the-border look, bake it in a terracotta pan or clean small flowerpots.

- 1 **cup** *each* **yellow cornmeal and all-purpose flour**
- 1 **tablespoon baking powder**
- ½ **teaspoon** *each* **salt and ground cumin**
- ¼ **teaspoon paprika**
- 1 **egg**
- 1 **cup milk**
- ¼ **cup salad oil**
- 1 **cup diced avocado (optional)**
- ⅓ **cup** *each* **diced red bell pepper and seeded, diced fresh or canned green chiles**
- ½ **cup shredded sharp Cheddar cheese**

In a large bowl, stir together cornmeal, flour, baking powder, salt, cumin, and paprika. In another bowl, lightly beat egg; stir in milk, oil, avocado (if used), bell pepper, chiles, and cheese. Stir milk mixture into dry ingredients just to moisten evenly.

Pour batter into a greased 8-inch square baking pan or 6 heavily greased 1-cup flowerpots or custard cups (if flowerpots have a hole in bottom, line bottom with a greased piece of foil). Arrange flowerpots on a baking sheet.

Bake bread in a 400° oven until a wooden pick inserted in center comes out clean (about 35 minutes for baking pan; 15 to 20 minutes for flowerpots). Let bread cool in pan or pots on a rack for 5 minutes; then turn out of pans onto rack and let cool completely. (If using flowerpots or a terracotta pan that you plan to give with bread, simply let bread cool completely in pots or pan.) Wrap airtight. Store at room temperature for up to 1 day; freeze bread made without avocado for up to 1 month. Makes 1 pan or 6 small pots cornbread.

BISCOTTI CRITTERS

(Pictured on facing page)

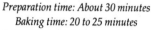

A feathered duck and a chubby chick are two of the winsome barnyard critters you can fashion from sweet biscotti dough.

Preparation time: *About 30 minutes*
Baking time: *20 to 25 minutes*
Storage time: *Best when freshly baked, but you may store up to 1 day at room temperature; up to 1 month in freezer*

Perfect for a springtime breakfast, these engaging critters are inspired by Italian *biscotti*. They're hard and crunchy—just right for breaking into chunks and dunking in coffee or warm milk. Make our bunny, or choose a duck or chubby chick.

- 2 **eggs**
- 1 **egg yolk**
- ¾ **cup plus 1 tablespoon sugar**
- ½ **cup (¼ lb.) butter or margarine, melted**
- 1 **teaspoon** *each* **vanilla and grated orange peel**
- 3 **cups all-purpose flour**
- 2 **teaspoons baking powder**
  Whole cloves (optional)
- 1 **egg white, lightly beaten**

In large bowl of an electric mixer, beat eggs, egg yolk, and ¾ cup of the sugar until thick and lemon-colored. Beat in butter, vanilla, and orange peel. In another bowl, mix flour and baking powder; add to butter mixture and blend well. Scrape dough onto a greased 14- by 17-inch baking sheet; press out to a thickness of ½ inch and shape as directed below. For eyes and whiskers, save small bits of dough to roll into balls or ropes; apply to dough base. Pinch surface with fingers to give texture; slash or score dough for definition. If desired, accent noses or eyes with cloves. Brush dough with egg white and sprinkle with remaining 1 tablespoon sugar.

Bake bread in a 350° oven until golden (20 to 25 minutes). Let cool on baking sheet for 5 minutes; transfer to a rack and let cool completely. Wrap airtight; store at room temperature for up to 1 day, in freezer for up to 1 month. Makes 1 large loaf.

BUNNY. Shape body 9 inches across at widest part, 7 inches high at center. Add dough for ears, tail, eyes, nose, and whiskers. Pinch body for texture.

DUCK. Shape body 10 inches across at widest part, 6 inches high at center. Use a ball of dough and a clove for eye. Pinch for feathered texture.

CHICK. Shape body 9½ inches across at widest part, 8 inches high at center. Slash to shape wing and tail; pinch wing for texture. Use a ball of dough and a clove for eye.

ZUCCHINI WHEAT BREAD

Preparation time: *About 20 minutes*
Baking time: *About 1 hour*
Storage time: *Up to 4 days at room temperature; up to 1 month in freezer*

Too much zucchini? Put some of the surplus to good use in these moist loaves—a delicious (and nutritious) treat for friends and family alike.

- 2½ **cups all-purpose flour**
- ½ **cup toasted wheat germ**
- 2 **teaspoons baking soda**
- 1 **teaspoon salt**
- ½ **teaspoon baking powder**
- 1 **cup finely chopped walnuts**
- 3 **eggs**
- 1 **cup** *each* **granulated sugar, firmly packed brown sugar, and salad oil**
- 1 **tablespoon maple flavoring**
- 2 **cups coarsely shredded zucchini (about 4 medium-size zucchini)**
- ⅓ **cup sesame seeds**

In a medium-size bowl, stir together flour, wheat germ, baking soda, salt, baking powder, and walnuts. Set aside.

In large bowl of an electric mixer, beat eggs until blended. Add sugars, oil, and maple flavoring; continue to beat until mixture is thick and foamy. Add flour mixture and stir just until blended. Stir in zucchini.

Divide batter between 2 greased, flour-dusted 5- by 9-inch loaf pans. Sprinkle sesame seeds over batter. Bake in a 350° oven until a wooden pick inserted in centers of loaves comes out clean (about 1 hour). Let cool in pans on racks for 10 minutes; then turn out onto racks. Let cool completely. Wrap airtight; store at room temperature for up to 4 days, in freezer for up to 1 month. Makes 2 loaves.

Depending on the shape you choose, easy-to-make Italian Biscotti
Critters (facing page) will look as cute as bunnies, ducks or chicks on an Easter brunch
table. To show off your critter's good looks, give it a ribbon bow tie
and nestle it in a tissue-lined basket tray, surrounded with fresh flowers or colored hard-
cooked eggs.

Festive Cranberry-Nut Bread

(Pictured on page 34)

Preparation time: About 20 minutes
Baking time: About 45 minutes for large loaf; about 30 minutes for small loaves
Storage time: Up to 2 days at room temperature; up to 1 month in freezer

Bright red cranberries give this breakfast bread its holiday appearance and tart, refreshing flavor.

- 2 **cups all-purpose flour**
- ½ **cup sugar**
- 1½ **teaspoons baking powder**
- ½ **teaspoon** *each* **salt and baking soda**
- 1 **egg, beaten**
- 10 **tablespoons orange juice**
- ¼ **cup butter or margarine, melted and cooled**
- 1 **cup fresh or frozen cranberries, cut in halves**
- ½ **cup coarsely chopped walnuts or pecans**

In a bowl, stir together flour, sugar, baking powder, salt, and baking soda until well blended. Make a well in center of flour mixture; add egg, orange juice, and butter. Stir just until dry ingredients are moistened. Stir in cranberries and walnuts.

Turn batter into a greased, flour-dusted 5- by 9-inch loaf pan or three 3½- by 5-inch loaf pans. Bake in a 350° oven until bread is golden brown on top and a wooden pick inserted in center comes out clean (about 45 minutes for large loaf; 30 minutes for small loaves). Let cool in pan(s) on a rack for 5 minutes, then turn out onto rack and let cool completely. Wrap airtight; store at room temperature for up to 2 days, in freezer for up to 1 month. Makes 1 large loaf or 3 small loaves.

Spicy Pumpkin Loaves

(Pictured on page 34)

Preparation time: 15 to 20 minutes
Baking time: About 1 hour and 10 minutes for large loaves; 40 minutes for small loaves
Storage time: Up to 2 days at room temperature; up to 1 month in freezer

Streamline your autumn baking with this moist, spicy bread. Each batch of batter makes four large

loaves or 12 mini-size loaves—some to keep, some to give away.

- 6 **eggs**
- 4½ **cups sugar**
- 1½ **cups salad oil**
- 1 **large can (29 oz.) solid-pack pumpkin**
- 5¼ **cups all-purpose flour**
- 1½ **teaspoons salt**
- 1 **tablespoon** *each* **baking soda, ground allspice, and ground cinnamon**
- 1½ **cups chopped walnuts or pecans**
- ¾ **cup raisins**

In a 5- to 6-quart bowl, lightly beat eggs. Add sugar, oil, and pumpkin; mix well. In another bowl, stir together flour, salt, baking soda, allspice, and cinnamon. Add to pumpkin mixture and stir just until blended; stir in walnuts and raisins.

Spoon batter into 4 greased, flour-dusted 4½- by 8½-inch loaf pans or twelve 3½- by 5-inch loaf pans (allow 3 cups batter for each large pan, 1 cup batter for each small pan). Bake in a 350° oven until a wooden pick inserted in center of bread comes out clean (about 1 hour and 10 minutes for large loaves; 40 minutes for small loaves). Let cool in pans on racks for 10 minutes; turn out onto racks and let cool completely. Wrap airtight; store at room temperature for up to 2 days, in freezer for up to 1 month. Makes 4 large or 12 small loaves.

Panettone

(Pictured on page 26)

Preparation time: 20 to 25 minutes
Baking time: 1½ to 1¾ hours for large mold; 45 minutes for small molds
Storage time: Up to 3 days at room temperature; up to 1 month in freezer

Traditional Milanese *panettone* is a yeast bread, but this quick version is every bit as delicious. To give it the traditional shape, bake it in a panettone mold. If you wish, you can give the mold as part of the gift; just remove the bread and wash the mold, then return the bread to the mold and wrap it.

- 2 **eggs**
- 2 **egg yolks**
- 1 **cup plus 2 tablespoons sugar**
- ¾ **cup (¼ lb. plus ¼ cup) butter or margarine, melted and cooled**
- 1½ **teaspoons** *each* **grated lemon peel, anise seeds, and anise extract**
- ⅓ **cup** *each* **pine nuts, raisins, and coarsely chopped mixed candied fruit**

    4 cups all-purpose flour
    1 tablespoon baking powder
    ¾ teaspoon salt
    1½ cups milk

In large bowl of an electric mixer, beat eggs, egg yolks, and sugar until thick and lemon-colored. Beat in butter; then add lemon peel, anise seeds, anise extract, pine nuts, raisins, and candied fruit. In another bowl, stir together flour, baking powder, and salt. Blend half the dry ingredients into egg mixture. Stir in half the milk; add remaining dry ingredients and mix well. Blend in remaining milk.

Pour batter into a greased, flour-dusted panettone or other 8-cup mold (or into two 4-cup molds). Bake in a 325° oven until bread is cracked and well browned on top and a slender skewer inserted in center comes out clean (1½ to 1¾ hours for large mold; 45 minutes for small molds). Let cool in mold(s) on a rack for 15 minutes; turn out onto rack and let cool completely. Wrap airtight; store at room temperature for up to 3 days, in freezer for up to 1 month. Makes 1 large loaf or 2 small loaves.

READY-BAKE BRAN MUFFINS

(Pictured on page 18)

Preparation time: 20 to 25 minutes
Baking time: 12 to 18 minutes
Storage time: Up to 2 weeks in refrigerator for batter; up to 1 day at room temperature, up to 1 month in freezer for baked muffins

Keep a bowl of this muffin batter on hand in your refrigerator, ready to bake into rich-tasting, fruit-dotted muffins at a moment's notice.

    3 cups whole bran cereal
    1 cup boiling water
    2 eggs, lightly beaten
    2 cups buttermilk
    ½ cup salad oil
    1 cup raisins, currants, snipped pitted dates, or chopped pitted prunes
    2½ teaspoons baking soda
    ½ teaspoon salt
    1 cup sugar
    2½ cups all-purpose flour

In a large bowl, mix bran cereal with boiling water, stirring to moisten evenly. Let cool. Add eggs, buttermilk, oil, and raisins; blend well. Mix baking soda, salt, sugar, and flour; stir into bran mixture.

Bake muffins right away; or refrigerate batter in a tightly covered container for up to 2 weeks. Stir batter to distribute fruit before using.

To bake, spoon batter into greased 2- to 2½-inch muffin cups, filling ⅔ to ¾ full. Bake in a 425° oven until tops of muffins spring back when lightly touched (12 to 18 minutes). Remove from pans and let cool completely on racks. Wrap airtight; store at room temperature for up to 1 day, in freezer for up to 1 month (thaw frozen muffins wrapped). On gift tag, suggest reheating muffins before serving: arrange on a baking sheet, cover loosely with foil, and heat in a 350° oven for about 10 minutes. Makes 2 to 3 dozen muffins.

SWEET MINI-MUFFINS

Preparation time: About 15 minutes
Baking time: 12 to 18 minutes
Storage time: Up to 1 day at room temperature; up to 1 month in freezer

Tiny muffins with a sweet, sparkling cinnamon-sugar coating make a charming gift. They're at their best served warm from the oven, so be sure to include reheating directions on your gift tag.

    ¼ cup butter or margarine, at room temperature
    ½ cup sugar
    1 egg
    2 cups all-purpose flour
    4 teaspoons baking powder
    ½ teaspoon *each* salt and ground nutmeg
    1 cup milk
      About ½ cup (¼ lb.) butter or margarine, melted
    2 teaspoons ground cinnamon mixed with ½ cup sugar

In a medium-size bowl, beat together the ¼ cup butter and the ½ cup sugar until blended, then beat in egg. Sift together flour, baking powder, salt, and nutmeg. Stir dry ingredients into butter mixture alternately with milk, blending well after each addition.

Spoon batter into greased 1½-inch muffin cups, filling ⅔ to ¾ full. Bake in a 375° oven until golden brown (12 to 18 minutes). Remove from pans. While muffins are still hot, dip each into melted butter, coating evenly; then roll in cinnamon-sugar mixture. Place on a plate and let cool completely. Wrap airtight; store at room temperature for up to 1 day, in freezer for up to 1 month (thaw frozen muffins unwrapped). On gift tag, suggest reheating muffins before serving: arrange on a baking sheet, cover loosely with foil, and heat in a 350° oven for about 10 minutes. Makes 3 dozen mini-muffins.

Heart-shaped cookie cutters, muffin tins, and cake pans make it easy
to say "I love you" with quick breads at a Valentine's Day breakfast. Shown here
(clockwise from right) are Buttermilk Scone Hearts (facing page),
Ready-bake Bran Muffins (page 17), and streusel-topped All-season Fruit Coffee Cake
(facing page). Present the breads in baskets lined with doilies or
napkins.

ALL-SEASON FRUIT COFFEE CAKE

(Pictured on facing page)

Preparation time: 20 to 30 minutes, depending on fruit used
Baking time: 50 to 60 minutes
Storage time: Up to 1 day at room temperature; up to 1 month in freezer

Blueberries, cherries, apricots, nectarines, peaches, plums, apples—you can use whatever fruit is in season to top this luscious, easy-to-make coffee cake. Plan on giving the baking pan along with the cake—we used a heart-shaped pan in the photo on the facing page.

 2 cups all-purpose flour
 1 cup sugar
 2 teaspoons baking powder
 1 teaspoon salt
 1½ teaspoons grated orange peel
 ½ cup (¼ lb.) firm butter or margarine
 2 eggs
 1 cup milk
 1 teaspoon vanilla
 3½ cups blueberries; pitted sweet cherries; pitted apricots, nectarines, or plums, sliced ½ inch thick; peeled, pitted peaches, sliced ½ inch thick; or peeled, cored apples, sliced ¼ inch thick
   Streusel Topping (recipe follows)

In a large bowl, stir together flour, sugar, baking powder, salt, and orange peel. Using a pastry blender or 2 knives, cut in butter until mixture resembles coarse meal. In another bowl, lightly beat eggs, then stir in milk and vanilla. Make a well in center of flour mixture and pour in egg mixture; stir just until moistened.

Spoon batter into a well-greased 1½-quart baking pan; arrange fruit of your choice evenly on top, pressing in lightly. Prepare Streusel Topping and scatter over fruit.

Bake in a 350° oven until a wooden pick inserted in center of cake comes out clean (50 to 60 minutes). Let cool completely in pan. Wrap airtight; store at room temperature for up to 1 day, in freezer for up to 1 month (thaw frozen cake wrapped). On gift tag, suggest reheating coffee cake before serving: bake, lightly covered with foil, in a 350° oven for about 10 minutes. Makes 1 coffee cake.

STREUSEL TOPPING. In a small bowl, combine ⅓ cup firmly packed **brown sugar,** ¼ cup **all-purpose flour,** and 1 teaspoon **ground cinnamon.** With your fingers, work in 2 tablespoons firm **butter** or margarine until well distributed. Stir in ½ cup chopped **almonds** or walnuts.

BUTTERMILK SCONE HEARTS

(Pictured on facing page)

Preparation time: About 20 minutes
Baking time: About 12 minutes
Storage time: Up to 1 day at room temperature; up to 1 month in freezer

Bake these British teatime favorites in heart shapes for special Valentine remembrances, or use your favorite cookie cutters to create fanciful shapes for any occasion. The buttery, fruit-laced dough goes together quickly for a last-minute gift.

 3 cups all-purpose flour
 ⅓ cup sugar
 2½ teaspoons baking powder
 ½ teaspoon baking soda
 ¾ teaspoon salt
 ¾ cup (¼ lb. plus ¼ cup) firm butter or margarine
 ¾ cup snipped pitted dates or currants
 1 teaspoon grated orange peel
 1 cup buttermilk
   About 1 tablespoon cream or milk
 ¼ teaspoon ground cinnamon mixed with 2 tablespoons sugar

In a large bowl, stir together flour, the ⅓ cup sugar, baking powder, baking soda, and salt. Using a pastry blender or 2 knives, cut in butter until mixture resembles coarse meal; stir in dates and orange peel. Make a well in center of butter-flour mixture; add buttermilk all at once. Stir with a fork until dough cleans sides of bowl.

With your hands, gather dough into a ball; turn out onto a lightly floured board. Roll or pat out ½ inch thick. Cut out dough with a 2½-inch heart-shaped cutter (or use another shape of your choice). Place scones 1½ inches apart on lightly greased baking sheets. Brush scones with cream; sprinkle lightly with cinnamon-sugar mixture.

Bake in a 425° oven until tops are lightly browned (about 12 minutes). Let cool completely on racks. Wrap airtight; store at room temperature for up to 1 day, in freezer for up to 1 month (thaw frozen scones wrapped). On gift tag, suggest reheating scones before serving: wrap in foil and heat in a 350° oven for about 10 minutes. Makes about 1½ dozen scones.

YEAST BREADS

Gifts of old-fashioned goodness from your oven

Nothing quite compares to the rich, yeasty aroma and flavor of fresh, made-from-scratch bread. And because few people today have the time to make yeast bread, it's all the more appreciated when you give it as a gift. The selection in this chapter goes beyond the ordinary, to include all shapes, flavors, and even colors. You can choose anything from whimsical little dove-shaped rolls to piquant red or green chile loaves to sweet, sugar-dusted *kugelhof* baked in a fancy mold. There are traditional holiday favorites, too— *stollen* for Christmas, hot cross buns for Easter.

You'll find these recipes adaptable: you can make a single lovingly shaped loaf or a whole breadbox full of little loaves. You can make the bread ahead and freeze it for giving later, or pull it straight from the oven and bundle it, warm and fragrant, into a gift basket. If you do choose to make your gift breads in advance, be sure to include re-heating instructions on the tag as noted on page 25. (See the Sunset book *Breads* for basic bread-making techniques.)

No matter what the season or occasion, when you give homemade bread, you're giving a gift of old-fashioned goodness that will be welcomed and enjoyed by anyone.

Molasses Pumpernickel Bread

♥ ♥ ♥

Preparation time: About 35 minutes, plus 2¼ hours for dough to rise
Baking time: 30 to 35 minutes
Storage time: Up to 1 day at room temperature; up to 1 month in freezer

A decoratively slashed crust and dark, rich color give this hearty bread a rustic appeal. You might present it with a selection of cheeses and perhaps some homemade salami (page 92).

> 2 tablespoons butter or margarine
> 2 cups milk
> 1½ teaspoons salt
> ½ cup dark molasses
> ½ cup warm water (about 110°F)
> 2 packages active dry yeast
> ⅓ cup firmly packed dark brown sugar
> 1½ cups whole bran cereal
> 3 cups rye flour
> About 4½ cups all-purpose flour
> 1 egg yolk beaten with 1 tablespoon water

Melt butter in a small pan; stir in milk, salt, and molasses. Set aside.

Pour warm water into a large bowl and stir in yeast and sugar until dissolved. Let stand until bubbly (about 15 minutes). Then add milk mixture, bran cereal, rye flour, and 2 cups of the all-purpose flour; beat until well blended.

Mix in about 1½ cups more all-purpose flour to make a stiff dough. Then knead on a floured board (or knead with a dough hook) until dough is smooth and satiny (10 to 15 minutes), adding more all-purpose flour as necessary.

Place dough in a greased bowl; turn to grease top. Cover with plastic wrap and let rise in a warm place until doubled (about 1½ hours).

Punch dough down and knead briefly on a floured board to release air. Divide into 2 equal portions and shape each into a smooth ball; flatten slightly.

Place each loaf on a greased baking sheet (at least 10 by 15 inches). Cover with plastic wrap and let rise in a warm place until almost doubled (about 45 minutes). With a razor blade or sharp floured knife, make ½-inch-deep slashes on tops of loaves, forming a ticktacktoe design. Brush with egg yolk mixture.

Bake in a 350° oven until bread is richly browned and sounds hollow when tapped (30 to 35 minutes). To bake both loaves in the same oven, stagger baking sheets on separate oven racks and switch their positions halfway through baking. Transfer loaves to racks and let cool completely. Wrap airtight; store at room temperature for up to 1 day, in freezer for up to 1 month. Makes 2 loaves.

Cheddar-Caraway Batter Bread

♥ ♥ ♥

Preparation time: About 20 minutes, plus 1½ hours for dough to rise
Baking time: About 55 minutes for tube pan; 45 minutes for loaf pans
Storage time: Up to 1 day at room temperature; up to 1 month in freezer

Here's a delicious time-saver—no kneading required! It's a cheese- and caraway-flavored batter bread to bake in loaf pans or a tube pan.

> 1 large can (12 oz.) evaporated milk (or 1½ cups half-and-half or light cream)
> 3 tablespoons sugar
> 3 tablespoons butter or margarine, cut into pieces
> 2 teaspoons *each* salt and caraway seeds
> ½ teaspoon garlic powder
> 1½ cups (6 oz.) shredded sharp Cheddar cheese
> 1 package active dry yeast
> ¼ cup warm water (about 110°F)
> 3¾ cups all-purpose flour
> 2 eggs

In a pan, combine evaporated milk, sugar, butter, salt, caraway seeds, garlic powder, and cheese. Over medium heat, stir and heat to about 110°F.

In a large bowl, sprinkle yeast over warm water and let stand for about 5 minutes to soften. Add milk mixture; beat in 1½ cups of the flour. Add eggs, 1 at a time, beating well after each addition; gradually beat in remaining 2¼ cups flour until batter is smooth. Cover with plastic wrap and let rise in a warm place until doubled (about 45 minutes).

Stir batter down and spoon into a generously greased 10-inch plain or decorative tube pan or two 4½- by 8½-inch loaf pans. Cover with plastic wrap and let rise in a warm place until almost doubled (about 45 minutes).

Bake in a 350° oven until browned (about 55 minutes for tube pan; about 45 minutes for loaf pans).

Let bread cool in pan(s) on a rack for 5 minutes; then turn out onto rack and let cool completely. Wrap airtight; store at room temperature for up to 1 day, in freezer for up to 1 month. Makes 1 large loaf or 2 small loaves.

CHILE BREAD

(Pictured on facing page)

Preparation time: 30 to 45 minutes, plus 2½ hours for dough to rise
Baking time: About 40 minutes
Storage time: Up to 1 day at room temperature; up to 1 month in freezer

Colored an earthy red or green with chile purée, this bread has an agreeable nip. Toasting brings out the aroma and flavor.

    Green or Red Chile Purée
    (directions follow)
  1 **package active dry yeast**
  ¼ **cup warm water (about 110°F)**
  ½ **cup milk**
  2 **tablespoons butter or margarine**
  1 **teaspoon salt**
  1 **tablespoon sugar**
  4½ **to 5 cups all-purpose flour**

Prepare chile purée of your choice and set aside.

In a large bowl, sprinkle yeast over warm water and let stand for about 5 minutes to soften. Meanwhile, in a 2- to 4-cup pan, heat milk and butter to 110°F. Add to yeast along with salt, sugar, chile purée, and 2 cups of the flour, stirring to blend well.

Stir in 1½ cups more flour until moistened, then beat vigorously until dough forms long, stretchy strands (about 10 minutes). With a dough hook, knead in 1 to 1½ cups more flour (or knead it in by hand on a floured board).

Place dough in a greased bowl and turn to grease top. Cover with plastic wrap and let rise in a warm place until doubled (about 1½ hours).

Punch dough down and knead briefly on a floured board to release air. Shape into a smooth loaf and place in a greased 5- by 9-inch loaf pan. Cover with plastic wrap and let rise in a warm place until dough has risen 1½ inches above pan rim (about 1 hour).

Bake in a 375° oven until golden brown (about 40 minutes). Turn out onto a rack and let cool completely. Wrap airtight; store at room temperature for up to 1 day, in freezer for up to 1 month. Makes 1 loaf.

GREEN CHILE PURÉE. In a blender or food processor, whirl 1 can (7 oz.) **diced green chiles** just until smooth. You should have ¾ cup. For hotter flavor, add ⅛ to ¼ teaspoon **ground red pepper** (cayenne).

RED CHILE PURÉE. In a 1½- to 2-quart pan, combine 2 ounces (about 6 large) **dried red New Mexico or California chiles** (stems and seeds removed) with 1½ cups **water.** Cover and simmer until chiles are very soft (about 15 minutes). In a blender or food processor, whirl chiles with 1 to 2 tablespoons of the cooking liquid until puréed (add more liquid if necessary). You should have about ½ cup purée. For hotter flavor, stir in 1 tablespoon **crushed dried hot red chiles.**

PARTY BREAD STICKS

(Pictured on front cover)

Preparation time: About 45 minutes, plus 15 minutes for dough to rise
Baking time: 15 to 20 minutes
Storage time: Up to 1 day at room temperature; up to 1 month in freezer

A bundle of homemade bread sticks is a welcome bring-along addition to a dinner party or a fun touch for a gift basket of cheeses or pasta fixings.

  3 **to 3½ cups all-purpose flour**
  1 **tablespoon sugar**
  1 **teaspoon salt**
  2 **packages active dry yeast**
  ¼ **cup olive oil or salad oil**
  1¼ **cups hot water (120° to 130°F)**
  1 **egg white beaten with 1 tablespoon water**
    Coarse (kosher-style) salt, toasted
    sesame seeds, or poppy seeds (optional)

In large bowl of an electric mixer, stir together 1 cup of the flour, sugar, salt, and yeast. Add oil, then gradually stir in hot water. Beat on medium speed for 2 minutes. Add ½ cup more flour and beat on high speed for 2 minutes. Mix in 1½ to 2 cups more flour to make a soft dough.

Scrape dough out onto a well-floured board and, with well-floured hands, work it into a smooth ball. With a sharp knife, cut into 20 equal pieces for 16-inch sticks (or 16 pieces for 20-inch sticks). Roll each piece of dough into a 16- or 20-inch rope; arrange ropes about 1 inch apart on oiled baking sheets, rolling to grease all sides.

Set bread sticks in a warm place, cover with plastic wrap, and let rise in a warm place until puffy (about 15 minutes). With a soft brush, paint each stick with egg white mixture. Sprinkle lightly with coarse salt or seeds; or leave plain. Bake in a 375° oven until lightly browned all over (15 to 20 minutes). Transfer to racks and let cool completely. Wrap airtight; store at room temperature for up to 1 day, in freezer for up to 1 month (thaw frozen bread sticks unwrapped). On gift tag, suggest recrisping bread sticks before serving: bake, uncovered, in a 300° oven for 5 minutes. Makes 16 or 20 extra-large bread sticks.

Nippy autumn days are perfect for baking red or green Chile Bread (facing page) or chile-seasoned Mexicana Cornbread (page 13). To give the breads a Southwest look, bake cornbread in terracotta pots; wrap yeast breads in earth-tone napkins or cornhusk "ribbons."

WHITE MINI-LOAVES

♥ ♥ ♥

Preparation time: About 30 minutes, plus 1½ hours for dough to rise
Baking time: 25 to 30 minutes
Storage time: Up to 2 days at room temperature;
up to 1 month in freezer

You can bake half a dozen of these golden little breads for friends in the time it takes to bake just one large loaf.

About 6 cups all-purpose flour
2 **tablespoons sugar**
1½ **teaspoons salt**
1 **package active dry yeast**
1 **cup** *each* **milk and water**
4½ **tablespoons butter or margarine**

In large bowl of an electric mixer, stir together 2 cups of the flour, sugar, salt, and yeast.

In a 1- to 2-quart pan, combine milk, water, and 3 tablespoons of the butter; heat to 110°F. Add milk mixture to flour mixture and stir to moisten; then beat on medium speed for 2 minutes. Add ¾ to 1 cup more flour to make a thick batter. Beat on high speed for 2 minutes. Mix in 2½ to 3 cups more flour to make a soft dough. Then knead on a floured board (or knead with a dough hook) until dough is smooth and elastic (about 10 minutes).

Place in a greased bowl; turn to grease top. Cover with plastic wrap and let rise in a warm place until doubled (about 1 hour).

Punch dough down and knead briefly on a floured board to release air. Divide into 6 equal pieces. Shape each into a loaf and place in a greased 3½- by 5-inch loaf pan. Cover loaves with plastic wrap and let rise in a warm place until almost doubled (20 to 30 minutes).

Melt remaining 1½ tablespoons butter and brush over loaves. Place pans slightly apart on a 12- by 15-inch baking sheet. Bake in a 375° oven until golden brown (25 to 30 minutes). Turn out onto racks and let cool completely. Wrap airtight; store at room temperature for up to 2 days, in freezer for up to 1 month. Makes 6 small loaves.

♥ HERB-CHEESE MINI-LOAVES

Follow directions for **White Mini-loaves,** but add 1 teaspoon *each* **dry basil, oregano leaves, and thyme leaves** and ½ teaspoon **garlic powder** to milk mixture. After brushing loaves with melted butter, sprinkle each evenly with 1 teaspoon grated **Parmesan cheese.**

TRICOLOR BRAID

♥ ♥ ♥

Preparation time: About 45 minutes, plus about 2 hours for dough to rise
Baking time: About 35 minutes
Storage time: Up to 1 day at room temperature; up to 1 month in freezer

This showstopper loaf makes a handsome gift for any occasion. Each slice is a mosaic of wheat, pumpernickel, and white bread.

2 **packages active dry yeast**
2⅓ **cups warm water (about 110°F)**
2 **tablespoons honey**
1½ **teaspoons salt**
¼ **cup butter or margarine, at room temperature**
About 5 cups all-purpose flour
¼ **cup dark molasses or dark corn syrup**
2 **tablespoons wheat germ**
1⅓ **cups whole wheat flour**
2 **tablespoons unsweetened cocoa**
1½ **teaspoons caraway seeds**
1⅓ **cups rye flour**
1 **egg yolk beaten with 1 tablespoon water**

In large bowl of an electric mixer, sprinkle yeast over warm water and let stand for about 5 minutes to soften. Stir in honey, salt, butter, and 2⅓ cups of the all-purpose flour and beat on high speed for 4 minutes. Divide batter into thirds (about 1¼ cups each) and put into 3 bowls.

For whole wheat bread: To dough in first bowl, add 2 tablespoons of the molasses; then beat in wheat germ and whole wheat flour. Knead on a floured board (or knead with a dough hook) until smooth (about 5 minutes), adding all-purpose flour as necessary. Place dough in a greased bowl; turn to grease top.

For pumpernickel bread: To dough in second bowl, add remaining 2 tablespoons molasses, cocoa, caraway seeds, and rye flour. Knead on a floured board (or knead with a dough hook) until smooth (about 5 minutes), adding all-purpose flour as necessary. Place dough in a second greased bowl; turn to grease top.

For white bread: To dough in third bowl, add 1⅓ cups all-purpose flour. Knead on a floured board (or knead with a dough hook) until smooth (about 5 minutes), adding all-purpose flour as necessary. Place dough in a third greased bowl; turn to grease top.

To continue, cover bowls with plastic wrap and let dough rise in a warm place until doubled (about 1 hour).

Punch doughs down and divide each in half. Roll each portion into a smooth 15-inch rope. For each loaf, place 1 white, 1 wheat, and 1 pumpernickel rope on a greased 14- by 17-inch baking sheet; braid loosely and pinch ends to seal, tucking them underneath. Cover lightly with plastic wrap and let rise in a warm place until doubled (about 1 hour).

Brush loaves with egg yolk mixture. Bake in a 350° oven until well browned (about 35 minutes). To bake both loaves in the same oven, stagger baking sheets on separate oven racks and switch their positions halfway through baking. Transfer loaves to racks and let cool completely. Wrap airtight; store at room temperature for up to 1 day, in freezer for up to 1 month. Makes 2 loaves.

CHALLAH

♥ ♥ ♥

Preparation time: 20 to 30 minutes, plus 2½ hours for dough to rise
Baking time: 30 to 35 minutes
Storage time: Up to 2 days at room temperature;
up to 1 month in freezer

Fragrant, tender *challah* has long-standing religious significance for the Jewish people, who enjoy it at Friday night Sabbath suppers and sometimes adorn it with a sugar glaze for holidays.

  1 **package active dry yeast**
1¼ **cups warm water (about 110°F)**
  1 **teaspoon salt**
 ¼ **cup *each* sugar and salad oil**
  2 **eggs, lightly beaten**
      Pinch of ground saffron (optional)
  5 **to 5½ cups all-purpose flour**
  1 **egg yolk beaten with 1 tablespoon water**
  1 **tablespoon sesame or poppy seeds**

In a large bowl, sprinkle yeast over warm water and let stand for about 5 minutes to soften. Then stir in salt, sugar, oil, eggs, and saffron (if used). Mix in about 4½ cups of the flour to make a stiff dough. Then knead on a floured board (or knead with a dough hook) until dough is smooth and satiny (10 to 20 minutes), adding more flour as necessary. Place dough in a greased bowl; turn to grease top. Cover with plastic wrap and let rise in a warm place until doubled (about 1½ hours). Punch dough down; knead briefly on a lightly floured board to release air. Set aside about ¾ cup dough and cover it.

Divide remaining dough into 4 equal portions; roll each between your hands to form a rope about 20 inches long. Place all 4 ropes lengthwise on a large greased baking sheet (at least 14 by 17 inches; or put 2 sheets together, overlapping ends and wrapping the overlap with foil). Pinch tops together, then braid ropes as follows: pick up rope on right, bring it over second rope, under third rope, and over fourth, as shown below left. Repeat, always starting with rope on right, until braid is complete. Pinch ends together and tuck under loaf.

Roll reserved dough into a rope about 15 inches long; cut into 3 pieces and make a small 3-strand braid. Lay on top center of large braid as shown below right. Cover with plastic wrap and let rise in a warm place until almost doubled (about 1 hour).

Using a soft brush or your fingers, spread egg yolk mixture evenly over braids; sprinkle with seeds. Bake in a 350° oven until golden brown (30 to 35 minutes). Transfer to a rack and let cool completely. Wrap airtight; store at room temperature for up to 2 days, in freezer for up to 1 month. Makes 1 loaf.

 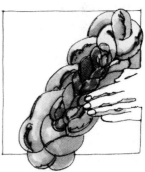

Shape *a 4-strand braid (left); then make a smaller 3-strand braid and center on top (right).*

TIPS FOR GIFT BREADS

When baking yeast breads to give as gifts, you'll want to follow these suggestions.

■ To store yeast breads, let them cool completely; then wrap in plastic wrap or a plastic bag to hold at room temperature, in foil and a plastic bag to store in the freezer. Thaw frozen breads wrapped unless your recipe specifies otherwise.

■ If the bread has a glaze, it's best to add it shortly before giving. You can glaze the bread at room temperature or when still frozen, but do make sure to let the glaze dry slightly before gift-wrapping.

■ Since many yeast breads taste better if reheated before serving, write out reheating instructions right on the gift tag.

To reheat yeast breads: Place bread or rolls on a baking sheet and cover loosely with foil (if glazed, reheat uncovered). Bake in a 350° oven until hot (10 to 15 minutes for rolls and small loaves; 15 to 20 minutes for large loaves).

Fancy tin, copper, or glass molds filled with a favorite bread or cake
can be given together as a unique gift on Mother's Day or Christmas, or at a wedding
shower. Choose (shown clockwise from right) fluted Panettone
(page 16), Fish-shaped Almond Loaves (facing page), Persimmon Pudding (page 40),
or Alsatian Kugelhof (facing page) in a tube mold or square pan.

FISH-SHAPED ALMOND LOAVES

(Pictured on facing page)

Preparation time: About 35 minutes, plus 2¾ hours for dough to rise
Baking time: About 35 minutes
Storage time: Up to 1 day at room temperature; up to 1 month in freezer

Baked in fish-shaped metal molds, these enchanting breads sport sliced-almond "scales" and a rich almond-paste filling. Using the same dough, you can make Alsatian Kugelhof in the traditional tube pan (or other plain or decorative pan).

Whichever version you choose, you might include the mold as part of the gift. If you do, be sure to unmold the baked bread, wash the mold, and then return the bread to the mold for gift-wrapping.

- ¾ **cup raisins**
- 1½ **tablespoons kirsch or lemon juice**
- 1 **package active dry yeast**
- ¼ **cup warm water (about 110°F)**
- ½ **cup (¼ lb.) butter or margarine, at room temperature**
- ½ **cup granulated sugar**
- 1 **teaspoon** *each* **grated lemon peel, vanilla, and salt**
- 3 **eggs**
- 3 **cups all-purpose flour**
- ½ **cup milk**
  Almond Filling (recipe follows)
  About 6 tablespoons sliced almonds
  Granulated or powdered sugar

In a small bowl, mix raisins with kirsch and set aside. In another small bowl, sprinkle yeast over warm water and let stand for about 5 minutes to soften. In a large bowl, beat butter, the ½ cup granulated sugar, lemon peel, vanilla, and salt until well blended; then add eggs, 1 at a time, mixing thoroughly after each addition. Stir in yeast. Add flour alternately with milk, mixing well after each addition. Beat dough vigorously for 5 minutes. Stir in raisin mixture. Cover with plastic wrap and let rise in a warm place until doubled (about 2 hours). Meanwhile, prepare Almond Filling and refrigerate as directed.

Generously butter 3 fish-shaped molds suitable for baking; each should have a 2½-cup capacity and be about 10 inches long. In bottom of each pan, overlap sliced almonds like fish scales, starting just behind the head; you'll need about 2 tablespoons almonds for each mold.

Beat dough down, then spoon about ⅙ of the dough into each mold; press dough gently with buttered fingers to make an even layer.

Lay a roll of Almond Filling on dough in each mold, pressing gently so dough oozes up against filling. Spoon remaining dough equally into molds, covering filling; with buttered fingers, press dough out to fill mold evenly and seal in filling. Cover with plastic wrap and let rise in a warm place until almost doubled (about 45 minutes).

Bake on lowest rack in a 350° oven until loaves are well browned (about 35 minutes). Let cool in molds for about 10 minutes, then invert onto a rack. Sprinkle with granulated or powdered sugar. Let cool completely. Wrap airtight; store at room temperature for up to 1 day, in freezer for up to 1 month. Makes 3 small loaves.

ALMOND FILLING. Smoothly blend ¼ cup **butter** or margarine (at room temperature) and ⅔ cup **powdered sugar**. Add ⅓ cup **all-purpose flour** and ½ cup **almond paste;** stir until crumbly and evenly mixed. Beat in 1 **egg white.** Cover and refrigerate until easy to handle (30 minutes to 1 hour). Shape into 3 rolls, each about 8 inches long; cover rolls of filling and refrigerate until ready to use.

♥ ALSATIAN KUGELHOF

(Pictured on facing page)

Prepare dough as directed for **Fish-shaped Almond Loaves,** but omit Almond Filling and add ⅓ cup coarsely chopped **blanched almonds** to dough along with raisins. Generously butter a 10-cup decorative tube pan or mold; arrange sliced almonds in bottom (you will need only ¼ cup sliced almonds). After dough has risen once, beat down and pour into prepared pan. Cover with plastic wrap and let rise in a warm place until dough almost reaches top of pan (about 1 hour).

Bake on lowest rack in a 350° oven until loaf is well browned (about 40 minutes). Let cool in pan on a rack for about 15 minutes; turn out onto rack and let cool completely. Sprinkle with granulated or powdered sugar. Wrap airtight; store at room temperature for up to 1 day, in freezer for up to 1 month. Makes 1 loaf.

Note: If desired, you may bake dough in 2 well-buttered 8- or 9-inch square baking pans. Spoon into pans, let rise as directed above, and bake in a 350° oven until golden brown (30 to 35 minutes).

Giant Pecan Rolls

Preparation time: About 35 minutes, plus 3½ hours for dough to rise
Baking time: 30 to 35 minutes
Storage time: Up to 2 days at room temperature; up to 1 month in freezer

Deliciously sticky with brown sugar syrup, these irresistible sweet rolls are so generously proportioned that just one or two will feed a small family.

- ⅔ **cup milk**
- 1¾ **cups sugar**
- ¾ **teaspoon salt**
- ¾ **cup (¼ lb. plus ¼ cup) butter or margarine**
- 2 **packages active dry yeast**
- ½ **cup warm water (about 110°F)**
  About 5½ cups all-purpose flour
- 2 **eggs**
  Brown Sugar–Nut Syrup (recipe follows)
- 1 **tablespoon ground cinnamon**
- 1 **cup coarsely chopped pecans**

In a 1- to 2-quart pan, combine milk, ¾ cup of the sugar, salt, and ½ cup of the butter (cut into small pieces). Heat, stirring, to 110°F. Set aside.

In a large bowl, sprinkle yeast over warm water and let stand for about 5 minutes to soften. Blend in milk mixture. Add 3 cups of the flour and stir to moisten. Beat with an electric mixer on medium speed for 5 minutes. Beat in 1 whole egg and 1 egg yolk (reserve remaining white); beat in 1 cup more flour. By hand, mix in 1 cup more flour. Then knead on a floured board (or knead with a dough hook) until dough is smooth and elastic (about 10 minutes), adding more flour as necessary.

Place dough in a greased bowl; turn to grease top. Cover with plastic wrap and let rise in a warm place until doubled (about 2 hours).

Punch dough down. Scrape out onto a lightly floured board and knead briefly to release air; let rest for 10 minutes. Meanwhile, prepare syrup. Roll out dough to make an 18- by 24-inch rectangle. Melt remaining ¼ cup butter; brush over dough.

Combine cinnamon and remaining 1 cup sugar; sprinkle evenly over dough, then sprinkle with pecans. Starting from an 18-inch side, roll up dough jelly roll style. Moisten edge of dough with water and pinch snugly to seal. With a sharp knife, cut roll crosswise into 6 equal slices. Arrange slices, cut side up, in syrup-coated pan. Cover lightly with plastic wrap; let rise in a warm place until doubled (about 1½ hours).

Brush rolls with reserved egg white beaten with 1 teaspoon water. Bake in a 350° oven until well browned (30 to 35 minutes). Immediately invert onto a tray. Let cool completely. Wrap airtight; store at room temperature for up to 2 days, in freezer for up to 1 month. On gift tag, suggest reheating rolls (see page 25). Makes 6 large rolls.

Brown Sugar–Nut Syrup. In a 1½- to 2-quart pan, combine ¼ cup **butter** or margarine, 2 tablespoons **water,** and 1 cup firmly packed **dark brown sugar.** Bring to a boil over high heat; boil for 1 minute. Immediately pour into a 9- by 13-inch baking pan; tilt pan so syrup forms an even layer. Arrange 1 cup **pecan halves,** flat side up, on syrup.

Surprise Bread Bundles

Preparation time: About 35 minutes, plus 2 hours for dough to rise and 2 hours to chill
Baking time: About 25 minutes
Storage time: Up to 1 day in refrigerator; up to 1 month in freezer

Tied with bright ribbons, these tender little cream cheese–filled breads make a delightful gift for any occasion. You need to chill the dough for easy handling, so start a day ahead—or even weeks ahead, since the bundles freeze well.

- 1 **package active dry yeast**
- ¼ **cup warm water (about 110°F)**
- ½ **cup (¼ lb.) butter or margarine, melted**
- ½ **cup half-and-half, light cream, or milk**
- 3 **tablespoons sugar**
- 3 **eggs**
- 4 **to 4½ cups all-purpose flour**
- 1 **teaspoon ground nutmeg**
- ½ **teaspoon salt**
  Cheese Filling (recipe follows)
- 1 **egg beaten with 1 tablespoon water**

In large bowl of an electric mixer, sprinkle yeast over warm water and let stand for about 5 minutes to soften. Mix butter, half-and-half, and sugar; add to yeast mixture with the 3 eggs, 2 cups of the flour, nutmeg, and salt. Stir to blend. Beat on medium speed for 2 minutes.

Mix in 2 cups more flour. Then knead on a floured board (or knead with a dough hook) until dough is smooth and elastic, adding more flour as necessary.

Place dough in a greased bowl; turn to grease top. Cover with plastic wrap and let rise in a warm place until doubled (about 1½ hours). Punch down; knead briefly, then wrap airtight and refrigerate for at least 2 hours or until next day. Meanwhile, prepare Cheese Filling.

Scrape dough out onto a floured board and knead briefly to release air. Divide into 16 equal portions; shape each into a 6- to 6½-inch circle. Place 2 to 2½ tablespoons of filling in center of each circle. Draw dough up around filling and pleat; pinch firmly just above filling, letting top of dough flare loosely. As you finish bundles, place them 2 inches apart on greased 10- by 15-inch baking sheets; cover lightly with plastic wrap and keep cold until all dough is shaped.

Place baking sheets with covered bundles in a warm place and let rise until puffy (about 30 minutes); then uncover. To seal firmly, lightly pinch pleats together again. Brush surfaces with egg mixture. Bake in a 350° oven until golden brown (about 25 minutes). Let cool completely on racks. Wrap airtight; store in refrigerator for up to 1 day, in freezer for up to 1 month.

Before giving, tie fabric ribbons around bundles. On gift tag, suggest reheating bundles (see page 25). Makes 16 bundles.

Cheese Filling. Beat together 2 large packages (8 oz. *each*) **cream cheese** (at room temperature); ½ cup **powdered sugar;** 1 **egg;** 2 teaspoons grated **orange peel;** and ¼ teaspoon **almond extract.** Stir in 1 cup **raisins** and ½ cup chopped **candied orange peel.** Use, or cover and refrigerate until next day.

Spring Dove Breads

Preparation time: About 1 hour, plus 2¼ hours for dough to rise
Baking time: 12 to 15 minutes
Storage time: Up to 1 day at room temperature; up to 1 month in freezer

To shape these little doves, you start with a rope of butter-rich dough. Just tie a knot for the body, add a small ball of dough for the head, and push in raisin eyes and an almond beak. As the dough rises and bakes, each bird takes on its own personality.

½	cup (¼ lb.) **butter** or **margarine**
6	tablespoons **whipping cream**
⅓	cup **sugar**
½	teaspoon **salt**
½	teaspoon **ground cardamom** or **nutmeg**
1	package **active dry yeast**
¼	cup **warm water** (about 110°F)
3	**eggs**
	About 4 cups **all-purpose flour**
24	**raisins**
12	whole blanched **almonds**
1	**egg yolk** beaten with 1 tablespoon **water**

In a 1- to 2-quart pan, melt butter; stir in cream, sugar, salt, and cardamom. Let cool to lukewarm.

Meanwhile, in large bowl of an electric mixer, sprinkle yeast over warm water; let stand for about 5 minutes to soften. Add cooled butter mixture, eggs, and 2 cups of the flour. Beat until well blended, then beat on medium speed for 2 minutes. Mix in about 1⅔ cups more flour to make a stiff dough. Then knead on a floured board (or knead with a dough hook) until dough is smooth and slightly elastic (about 10 minutes), adding more flour as necessary. Place in a greased bowl; turn to grease top. Cover dough with plastic wrap and let rise in a warm place until doubled (about 1½ hours).

Punch dough down and knead briefly on a lightly floured board to release air. Divide into 12 equal portions. Pinch off a ¾-inch ball of dough from each portion and set aside for dove heads.

To shape each dove body, roll 1 large portion of dough into a 9-inch-long rope measuring ½ inch wide at 1 end, 1 inch wide at other end. Tie an overhand knot at thin end of rope to make body. For tail, make several slashes in wide end of rope to resemble feathers, as shown below left. As dove bodies are shaped, place them at least 2 inches apart on greased baking sheets; cover lightly with plastic wrap and keep cold until all are shaped.

Shape reserved balls of dough for dove heads, forming them into smooth teardrops. Settle narrow ends of heads into cavities of dough knots; press down to secure. Make small slashes on each side of heads and insert raisins for eyes. At front of each head, make a small slash and insert wide end of almond for beak, as shown below right. Cover doves lightly with plastic wrap and let rise in a warm place until puffy (about 45 minutes).

Before baking, push raisins and almonds back into heads to secure. Brush rolls all over with egg yolk mixture. Bake in a 375° oven until golden (12 to 15 minutes). Transfer to racks and let cool completely. Wrap airtight; store at room temperature for up to 1 day, in freezer for up to 1 month. On gift tag, suggest reheating rolls (see page 25). Makes 1 dozen rolls.

***Knot** dough rope for dove body and slash wide end of tail (left); add raisin eyes and almond beak to dove head (right).*

Packaging—Pretty & Practical

Imaginative packaging can transform the gifts from your kitchen into delightful personalized offerings that will be long remembered. Why not offer homemade truffles in a brightly colored Chinese-food carton, or a little cake in a straw basket? Personalize store-bought jars, tins, and baskets with stenciled or rubber-stamped designs, or with whimsical stickers. On this page, you'll find a variety of ideas for packaging and decorating your gifts.

DRESSING UP STORE-BOUGHT CONTAINERS

■ **Paper bags** are perfect containers for anything from popcorn to cookies. You can buy colored and patterned bags, with or without handles, in many stationery and paper specialty shops. The plain brown lunch sacks sold at grocery stores make fine gift bags, too—just decorate them with stencils, stickers, or rubber stamps (see page 77). For a special touch, make a "window bag" as shown on the facing page: cut out a square, diamond, or other shape in the front of the bag, then tape a piece of clear cellophane inside. Fasten bag tops with a colorful metal or wooden clip. Or leave the bag open and line it with bright tissue paper, letting the tissue peek out from the bag's top.

■ **Baskets**—a perennial favorite —come in all shapes, sizes, even colors. Almost any basket looks pretty when cushioned with excelsior (as shown on the facing page) or Easter grass or lined with a colorful cloth or paper napkin.

Or try stenciling or stamping designs on the basket, or weaving a ribbon around the edge or handle or between the slats.

■ **Tins,** available in an enticing array of shapes, sizes, colors, and patterns, are delightful gifts in themselves. Perfect for cookies, candy, nuts, and even cakes, they help keep goodies fresh and are an ideal choice for mailing. To make a really individual container, buy a solid-color tin and decorate it with stickers like the toy soldiers shown in the photo.

■ **Boxes & cartons** are available in many styles and materials. Some stationery and specialty shops carry the familiar wire-handled Chinese-food cartons in bright colors. You'll also find decorated cartons made of plastic or heavy waxed cardboard as well as plain or decorated wooden boxes. To make any box more special, line the inside top and bottom with fabric or paper as shown on page 58. A "window box" is a lovely container for a cake: simply cut a window in the top of a cardboard bakery box and cover it with clear cellophane as for window bags.

■ **Bottles & jars** can be beautiful gifts all on their own (for examples, see pages 71 and 87)—but if you'd like to dress them up, a fluffy bow and a pretty purchased or handmade label are all that's needed. For extra-special treatment, cover a jar lid with a lacy paper doily or a circle of wrapping paper, tying it in place with ribbon, twine, or silk cord. Or use a cloth napkin tied with a half-bow of raffia, as shown on page 63. (Double-faced tape on the lid and a rubber band under the tie help hold cloth or paper in place.)

To create a coordinated package, make a matching lid-cover and tag. Cut a circle of fabric with pinking shears as we did at right; for a soft look, give the lid a light padding of polyester stuffing before tying on the fabric. To make the tag, iron a small rectangle of pinked fabric onto an index card using fusible web; glue on a smaller piece of paper (stamped or stenciled, if you wish).

MAKING YOUR OWN WRAPPINGS & LABELS

■ **A decorative tube** is a quick and original way to present candies, nuts, or a stack of little cookies. Simply wrap an empty cardboard tube from a paper towel roll in pretty paper and tie at both ends with ribbon or silk cord (or wrap with cord as shown at right). Seal with a gold notary seal or sticker, if you wish.

■ **Heat-sealing** breads, cakes, or cookies with plastic wrap shows them off and keeps them fresh. You can seal food as is, in a foil pan, or on a heavy cardboard base. First cover the food with a piece of heavy plastic wrap just large enough to overlap the edges at the bottom; pull the plastic gently across the top and fold the ends neatly underneath. Preheat oven to 300°. Set a piece of brown wrapping paper on the oven rack or on a baking sheet, then set the wrapped food on the paper; heat for 5 to 10 seconds to seal. Let cool briefly, then tie with a ribbon.

■ **Labels & tags** are a must for any package. Use purchased tags or stickers or make them yourself (see page 77).

**Eye-catching packaging adds the finishing touch to your food gifts.
Ideas here include stenciled or beribboned baskets, tins brightened with jaunty stickers,
decorated or peek-through window bags, a paper cookie or candy tube,
jars topped with doilies or fabric, and an array of delightful handmade labels and tags
(see page 77).**

31

Almond Bear Claws

♥ ♥ ♥

Preparation time: About 20 minutes, plus about 24 hours for dough to rise (1 day in refrigerator, 20 minutes after shaping)
Baking time: About 15 minutes
Storage time: Up to 2 days at room temperature; up to 1 month in freezer

Rich with almonds and butter, these professional-looking bear claws are easy to make with our refrigerator dough and streamlined technique.

- 1 cup (½ lb.) **butter** or margarine
- 1 package **active dry yeast**
- ¼ cup **warm water** (about 110°F)
- 3 **egg yolks**
- ¼ cup **sugar**
- ½ teaspoon **salt**
- 1 small can (5 oz.) **evaporated milk**
- 3⅓ cups **all-purpose flour**
  Almond Filling (recipe follows)
- 1 **egg white**, lightly beaten
  About ¾ cup sliced **almonds**
  Sugar

Melt butter, then let cool to 110°F. In a bowl, sprinkle yeast over warm water and let stand for about 5 minutes to soften. Stir in egg yolks, the ¼ cup sugar, salt, evaporated milk, and cooled butter.

Place flour in a large bowl, pour in yeast mixture, and beat well. Cover with plastic wrap and refrigerate for at least a day or up to 3 days. Prepare Almond Filling and refrigerate as directed.

To shape bear claws, punch dough down and knead briefly on a floured board to release air. Roll out into a 13½- by 27-inch rectangle, using a ruler to straighten edges. Cut dough lengthwise into 3 strips, each 4½ inches wide. Divide filling into 3 portions; on a floured board, roll each portion into a 27-inch rope. Lay an almond rope in center of each dough strip; then flatten rope slightly.

Fold long sides of each strip over filling. Cut each filled strip into 6 pieces, each 4½ inches long. Arrange, seam side down, on 3 greased 12- by 15-inch baking sheets. Using a floured sharp knife, make a row of cuts ¾ inch apart halfway across each piece, as shown at right. Then curve each bear claw so cut pieces fan out, as shown.

Brush egg white over bear claws; top with sliced almonds and sprinkle lightly with sugar. Let rise, uncovered, in a warm place until puffy (about 20 minutes).

Bake in a 375° oven until golden brown (about 15 minutes). Transfer to a rack and let cool completely. Wrap airtight; store at room temperature for up to 2 days, in freezer for up to 1 month. On

gift tag, suggest reheating bear claws (see page 25). Makes 1½ dozen bear claws.

Almond Filling. In a bowl, smoothly blend ½ cup (¼ lb.) **butter** or margarine (at room temperature) with 1⅓ cups **powdered sugar.** Add ⅔ cup **all-purpose flour** and 1 can or package (8 oz.) **almond paste.** Stir until crumbly and evenly mixed; then beat in 1 teaspoon grated **lemon peel** and 2 **egg whites.** Stir in ¾ cup finely chopped **almonds.** Cover and refrigerate until easy to handle (30 minutes to 1 hour) or for up to 3 days.

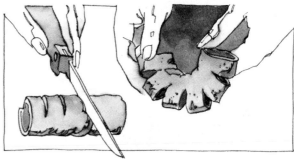

Make *row of cuts across each piece of dough (left); curve each piece so "claws" fan out (right).*

Dresden-style Stollen

(Pictured on page 34)

♥ ♥ ♥

Preparation time: 35 to 45 minutes, plus 2 to 2¼ hours for dough to rise
Baking time: 20 to 25 minutes
Storage time: Up to 1 day at room temperature; up to 1 month in freezer

In Germany, it's a Christmas tradition to bake a sugar-dusted *stollen* as a gift for friends. Chock-full of fruits and nuts, this version makes holiday breakfasts extra special.

- ½ cup **milk**
- 1 cup (½ lb.) **butter** or margarine
- ½ cup **granulated sugar**
- 2 packages **active dry yeast**
- ½ cup **warm water** (about 110°F)
- ½ teaspoon **salt**
- 1 teaspoon *each* grated **lemon peel** and **almond extract**
  About 5¼ cups **all-purpose flour**
- 2 **eggs**
- ⅓ cup finely chopped **candied orange peel**
- ½ cup *each* dark **raisins**, golden **raisins**, **currants**, and slivered **almonds**
- 1 **egg white** beaten with 1 teaspoon **water**
- ¼ cup **butter** or margarine, melted
- ⅓ cup **powdered sugar**

In a small pan, combine milk, the 1 cup butter, and granulated sugar. Heat to scalding (120°F) over medium low heat, stirring to dissolve sugar and melt butter. Let cool to lukewarm.

In a large bowl, sprinkle yeast over warm water and let stand for about 5 minutes to soften. Add cooled milk mixture, salt, lemon peel, almond extract, and 3 cups of the flour; beat until well blended. Add eggs, 1 at a time, beating well after each addition. Gradually stir in orange peel, raisins, currants, almonds, and 2 cups more flour.

Scrape dough out onto a floured board and knead until smooth and satiny (about 10 minutes), adding more flour as necessary. Place dough in a greased bowl; turn to grease top. Cover with plastic wrap and let rise in a warm place until doubled (about 1½ hours).

Punch dough down. Knead briefly on a floured board to release air, then divide in half. Place each portion on a lightly greased 12- by 15-inch baking sheet and shape into a 7- by 9-inch oval ¾ inch thick. Brush with some of the egg white mixture. Crease each oval lengthwise, slightly off center; fold so top edge lies an inch back from bottom edge. Brush with remaining egg white mixture. Cover with plastic wrap; let rise in a warm place until almost doubled (35 to 45 minutes).

Bake in a 375° oven until richly browned (20 to 25 minutes). To bake both loaves in the same oven, stagger baking sheets on separate oven racks and switch their positions halfway through baking. Brush baked loaves evenly with the ¼ cup melted butter and sift powdered sugar over tops. Return to oven and bake for 3 more minutes. Transfer to racks and let cool completely. Wrap airtight; store at room temperature for up to 1 day, in freezer for up to 1 month. On gift tag, suggest reheating loaves (see page 25). Makes 2 loaves.

CANDY CANE TWISTS

(Pictured on page 34)

♥ ♥ ♥

Preparation time: About 45 minutes, plus 2 to 2¼ hours for dough to rise
Baking time: About 20 minutes
Storage time: Up to 1 day at room temperature; up to 1 month in freezer

Swirled with red candied cherries, this sweet Christmas bread in a whimsical candy cane shape makes a cheery breakfast treat.

- 2 **packages active dry yeast**
- ½ **cup warm water (about 110°F)**
- 1 **cup warm milk (about 110°F)**

- 6 **tablespoons sugar**
- ½ **cup (¼ lb.) butter or margarine, at room temperature**
- 2 **teaspoons salt**
- 1 **teaspoon ground cardamom**
- 4 **eggs**
- 2 **teaspoons grated lemon peel**
  About 7 cups all-purpose flour
  Cherry-Almond Filling (recipe follows)

In large bowl of an electric mixer, sprinkle yeast over warm water and let stand for about 5 minutes to soften. Stir in milk, sugar, butter, salt, cardamom, eggs, and lemon peel. Beat in 4 cups of the flour, a cup at a time. Then beat on medium speed for 3 minutes, scraping bowl frequently.

Mix in 2½ cups more flour to make a soft dough. Then knead on a floured board (or knead with a dough hook) until dough is smooth (5 to 10 minutes), adding more flour as necessary.

Place dough in a greased bowl; turn to grease top. Cover with plastic wrap and let rise in a warm place until doubled (about 1½ hours). Meanwhile, prepare Cherry-Almond Filling.

Punch dough down and knead briefly on a floured board to release air. Divide into 3 equal portions. Roll each portion into a 6- by 20-inch rectangle. Crumble ⅓ of the filling over each rectangle, scattering it over dough to within 1 inch of edges. Starting with a long side, roll up dough tightly, jelly roll style. Moisten edge with water; pinch to seal.

Using a floured sharp knife, cut each roll in half lengthwise; carefully turn cut sides up. Loosely twist half-rolls around each other, keeping cut sides up. Carefully transfer each twist to a greased, flour-dusted baking sheet and shape into a cane. Cover lightly with plastic wrap and let rise in a warm place until puffy (35 to 45 minutes).

Bake in a 350° oven until lightly browned (about 20 minutes). Transfer loaves to racks and let cool completely. Wrap airtight; store at room temperature for up to 1 day, in freezer for up to 1 month. On gift tag, suggest reheating loaves (see page 25). Makes 3 loaves.

CHERRY-ALMOND FILLING. In large bowl of an electric mixer, beat ½ cup (¼ lb.) **butter** or margarine (at room temperature), ½ cup **all-purpose flour,** and ¼ cup **sugar** until smooth. Stir in 1⅓ cups finely chopped **blanched almonds,** 1 cup chopped **red candied cherries,** 1 teaspoon grated **lemon peel,** and 1½ teaspoons **almond extract.** Cover and refrigerate.

A loaf of homemade bread decorated with greenery and ribbons
is a special way to say "Merry Christmas." Quick-to-make choices (shown at center) are
Spicy Pumpkin Loaves or Festive Cranberry-Nut Bread (both on page 16).
Fancy sweet yeast breads include (left to right) Kardemummakrans (facing page),
Candy Cane Twists (page 33), or Dresden-style Stollen (page 32).

KARDEMUMMAKRANS

(Pictured on facing page)

Preparation time: About 30 minutes, plus 2 to 2½ hours for
dough to rise
Baking time: About 30 minutes
Storage time: Up to 2 days at room temperature;
up to 1 month in freezer

A Christmas tradition from Sweden, this festive braided bread gets dressed up for the holidays with a drizzle of icing and a sprinkle of cherries.

- 1 **package active dry yeast**
- ¼ **cup warm water (about 110°F)**
- 2½ **cups warm milk (about 110°F)**
- ¾ **cup (¼ lb. plus ¼ cup) butter or margarine, melted and cooled**
- 1 **egg**
- ½ **teaspoon salt**
- 1 **cup sugar**
- 1½ **teaspoons ground cardamom**
- 8 **to 9 cups all-purpose flour**
- **Icing (recipe follows)**
- **Red or green candied cherries**

In a large bowl, sprinkle yeast over warm water and let stand for about 5 minutes to soften. Stir in milk, butter, egg, salt, sugar, and cardamom.

Mix in 7½ cups of the flour to form a stiff dough. Then knead on a floured board (or knead with a dough hook) until dough is smooth and elastic (about 10 minutes), adding more flour as necessary. Place dough in a greased bowl, turn to grease top, cover with plastic wrap, and let rise in a warm place until almost doubled (1½ to 2 hours).

Punch dough down and knead briefly on a floured board to release air. Divide into 9 equal portions; roll each into a rope 18 inches long. Place 3 ropes on a greased baking sheet, pinch tops together, and braid loosely. Form braid into a ring, pinching ends together. Repeat to make 2 more rings. Cover with plastic wrap and let rise in a warm place until almost doubled (about 30 minutes).

Bake in a 350° oven until loaves are medium brown (about 30 minutes). Transfer loaves to a rack and let cool completely. Wrap airtight; store at room temperature for up to 2 days, in freezer for up to 1 month.

Before giving, prepare Icing and drizzle over loaves; decorate with cherries. Let Icing dry slightly before wrapping loaves. On gift tag, suggest reheating loaves (see page 25). Makes 3 loaves.

ICING. Stir together 2 cups **powdered sugar,** ¼ cup **milk,** and 1 teaspoon **lemon extract** until smooth.

HOT CROSS BUNS

Preparation time: 20 to 30 minutes, plus 2 hours for dough to rise
Baking time: 15 to 18 minutes
Storage time: Up to 1 day at room temperature; up to 1 month in freezer

These delicious little buns, each topped with a cross of lemon-flavored frosting, make a delightful Easter gift.

- 1 **package active dry yeast**
- ¼ **cup warm water (about 110°F)**
- 1 **cup warm milk (about 110°F)**
- 2 **tablespoons butter or margarine**
- ⅓ **cup sugar**
- ¾ **teaspoon** *each* **salt and ground cinnamon**
- ¼ **teaspoon** *each* **ground cloves and nutmeg**
- 2 **eggs**
- ¾ **cup currants**
- ¼ **cup finely diced candied orange peel or citron**
- **About 4½ cups all-purpose flour**
- 1 **egg yolk beaten with 1 tablespoon water**
- **Lemon Frosting (recipe follows)**

In a large bowl, sprinkle yeast over warm water and let stand for about 5 minutes to soften. Stir in milk, butter, sugar, salt, cinnamon, cloves, and nutmeg. Beat in eggs. Stir in currants, orange peel, and about 4 cups of the flour to make a soft dough. Then knead on a floured board (or knead with a dough hook) until dough is smooth and satiny (10 to 20 minutes), adding more flour as necessary. Place dough in a greased bowl and turn to grease top; cover with plastic wrap and let rise in a warm place until doubled (about 1½ hours).

Punch dough down and divide into 24 equal pieces; shape each into a smooth ball. Grease and flour-dust two 9-inch round cake pans; place 12 balls in each pan, spacing evenly. Brush balls gently with egg yolk mixture. Cover lightly with plastic wrap and let rise in a warm place until doubled (about 35 minutes).

Bake in a 375° oven until lightly browned (15 to 18 minutes). Turn out of pans onto racks; let cool completely. Wrap airtight; store at room temperature for up to 1 day, in freezer for up to 1 month. Before giving, prepare frosting; with a spoon or the tip of a knife, drizzle frosting over each bun to make a small cross. Let frosting dry slightly before wrapping buns. On gift tag, suggest reheating buns (see page 25). Makes 2 dozen buns.

LEMON FROSTING. Stir together 1 cup **powdered sugar,** 2 teaspoons **lemon juice,** and 1 teaspoon **water** until smooth.

CAKES & COOKIES

Traditional favorites & new discoveries

Who wouldn't be delighted to receive a fresh, home-baked cake or a tinful of brightly decorated cookies? Cakes and cookies have the kind of universal appeal that makes them sure winners as gifts any time. For those who like their goodies simple and straightforward, this chapter offers the ultimate chocolate chip cookie (and its white chocolate chip counterpart), as well as old-fashioned pound cake enlivened with liqueur. Traditionalists will love our delicious versions of such favorites as thumbprint cookies and fudge brownies, while adventurous souls might like a super-rich Italian ricotta cake or a French Almond Cake "gift-wrapped" in marzipan and topped with ribbons of dark chocolate. Though most of our cakes and cookies are good any time, some are especially appropriate for holidays; try Gingerbread Cutouts for Christmas or an Almond Fudge Cake for Mother's Day.

You'll want to give some of the treats in this chapter soon after they're baked, but others—Panfortinas, Applesauce Fruitcake, and Nürnberger Lebkuchen, for example—are ideal candidates for mailing to friends and family far away. For an especially original gift, you might make one of our "traveling" cakes the centerpiece of a complete birthday-in-a-box, as shown on page 47.

RICOTTA CRUMB CAKE

Preparation time: 45 to 60 minutes
Baking time: About 45 minutes
Storage time: Up to 2 days in refrigerator

This Sicilian-inspired, cheesecakelike dessert features a buttery crumb topping and a creamy filling studded with chunks of chocolate and pine nut brittle.

> Almond Crumb Crust (recipe follows)
> ⅓ cup granulated sugar
> ⅔ cup pine nuts or slivered almonds
> 3½ cups (1¾ lbs.) ricotta cheese
> 2 tablespoons light rum or ½ teaspoon rum flavoring
> ¾ cup granulated sugar
> 4 ounces semisweet chocolate, coarsely chopped, or ⅔ cup semisweet chocolate chips
> Powdered sugar

Prepare Almond Crumb Crust mixture and set aside.

Place the ⅓ cup granulated sugar in a wide, heavy frying pan and set over medium heat. Cook, shaking pan frequently, until sugar liquefies and turns golden. Stir in pine nuts; then immediately turn out into a buttered shallow pan. With a whole uncut lemon or a buttered spoon, press mixture to flatten slightly. Let cool; break into ½-inch pieces.

Mix ricotta, rum, and the ¾ cup granulated sugar until blended. Stir in chocolate and pine nut brittle.

Spoon half the Almond Crumb Crust mixture into a buttered 10-inch cheesecake pan with a removable bottom, piling it slightly higher around edges (do not press firmly). Pour ricotta mixture into center, leaving about a 1-inch border around edges. Spoon remaining crust mixture over top all the way to edges, then gently pat down to form an almost flat top.

Bake in a 350° oven until lightly browned (about 45 minutes). Let cool completely in pan on a rack. Remove pan sides; then carefully lift cake from pan bottom, loosening with a knife if necessary. Wrap airtight and store in refrigerator for up to 2 days. Before giving, sprinkle cake with powdered sugar. Makes 1 (10-inch) cake.

ALMOND CRUMB CRUST. Spread ⅔ cup **blanched almonds** in a shallow baking pan and toast in a 350° oven until golden (about 8 minutes), shaking pan frequently. Then whirl in a blender or food processor until finely ground.

In a large bowl, stir together ground almonds, 3¼ cups **all-purpose flour,** 1 tablespoon **baking powder,** and ⅔ cup firmly packed **brown sugar.** With a pastry blender, cut in ½ cup (¼ lb.) plus 6 tablespoons firm **butter** or margarine until fine crumbs form. Beat together 1 **egg** and 1 teaspoon **vanilla,** pour over dry ingredients, and toss together with a fork just until evenly moistened. Do not overmix; mixture should remain crumbly.

LEMON LOAF CAKE

Preparation time: About 20 minutes
Baking time: 40 to 45 minutes for large cake; 25 to 30 minutes for small cakes
Storage time: Up to 4 days at room temperature; up to 1 month in freezer

Here's an old-fashioned favorite to enjoy in any season. While it's hot from the oven, you poke it with a skewer until it's full of holes, then drizzle it with a sweet, lemony glaze. When cooled, it's easy to slice and has a fine, even texture, much like pound cake.

> 1½ cups all-purpose flour
> 1 cup sugar
> 1 teaspoon baking powder
> ½ teaspoon salt
> 2 eggs
> ½ cup *each* milk and salad oil
> 1½ teaspoons grated lemon peel
> Lemon Glaze (recipe follows)

In a large bowl, stir together flour, sugar, baking powder, and salt. In a small bowl, lightly beat eggs, then beat in milk, oil, and lemon peel. Add liquid mixture to flour mixture and stir just until blended.

Pour batter into a greased, flour-dusted 5- by 9-inch loaf pan or three 3½- by 5-inch loaf pans. Bake in a 350° oven until a wooden pick inserted in center of cake comes out clean (40 to 45 minutes for large cake; 25 to 30 minutes for small cakes).

When cake is done, use a long wooden skewer to poke numerous holes all the way to bottom. Prepare Lemon Glaze; drizzle hot glaze evenly over cake, letting it soak in slowly. Let cool in pan(s) on a rack for 15 minutes; turn out onto rack and let cool completely. Wrap airtight; store at room temperature for up to 4 days, in freezer for up to 1 month. Makes 1 large cake or 3 small cakes.

LEMON GLAZE. In a small pan, combine 4½ tablespoons **lemon juice** and ⅓ cup **sugar.** Stir over medium heat until sugar is dissolved.

LIQUEUR POUND CAKE

(Pictured on facing page)

♥ ♥ ♥

Preparation time: About 20 minutes
Baking time: About 50 minutes
Storage time: Up to 2 weeks in a cool place; up to 1 month in refrigerator; up to 6 months in freezer

These rich and tender-textured cakes, flavored with rum or sweet liqueur, are an ideal gift for mailing to loved ones in distant places.

- 1½ cups (¾ lb.) **butter** or **margarine**, at room temperature
- 1 box (1 lb.) **powdered sugar**
- 6 **eggs**
- 1 teaspoon **vanilla**
- 2¾ cups **cake flour**
  Liqueur Syrup (recipe follows)

In large bowl of an electric mixer, beat butter until creamy. Sift powdered sugar; gradually add to butter, beating until mixture is light and fluffy. Add eggs, 1 at a time, beating well after each addition. Beat in vanilla; gradually mix in flour.

Scrape batter into 4 greased, flour-dusted 3½-by 7-inch loaf pans. Smooth top of batter. Bake in a 300° oven until a wooden pick inserted in center of cake comes out clean (about 50 minutes). Meanwhile, prepare Liqueur Syrup.

Let cakes cool in pans on a rack for 5 minutes. Run a knife around edges of each pan and turn cake out; immediately return cake to pan. With a slender skewer or a fork, poke numerous holes, about 1 inch apart, all the way to the bottom of cake. Immediately pour an equal amount of syrup over each cake. Let cool on a rack until cakes have completely absorbed syrup (about 1 hour).

Remove cakes from pans; wrap airtight. Store cakes in a cool place for up to 2 weeks, in refrigerator for up to 1 month, or in freezer for up to 6 months. On gift tag, note that cake should be served at room temperature. Makes 4 small cakes.

LIQUEUR SYRUP. In a 2- to 3-quart pan, combine 2 cups **sugar,** ½ cup **light corn syrup,** and ¾ cup **water.** Set over medium-high heat and stir slowly until mixture comes to a simmer. Continue heating, without stirring, until mixture boils. Cover and continue to boil until sugar is dissolved and liquid is clear—about 1 minute. (If you don't cover pan and if you stir while syrup boils, crunchy sugar crystals will form in the finished cake.)

Remove from heat, uncover, and let stand until slightly cooled (5 minutes). Stir in 1¼ cups **rum** or almond-, hazelnut-, or orange-flavored liqueur.

ALMOND FUDGE CAKE

(Pictured on page 42)

♥ ♥ ♥

Preparation time: About 30 minutes (without Chocolate Walls)
Baking time: About 30 minutes
Storage time: Up to 2 days in refrigerator; up to 1 month in freezer

For an extra-special finish, give this fudgy cake thin chocolate "walls" and a lacy powdered sugar topping, or just add a dark chocolate glaze.

- 1 teaspoon **instant coffee powder**
- 2 tablespoons **hot water**
- 4 ounces **semisweet chocolate,** melted
- 3 **eggs,** separated
- ½ cup (¼ lb.) **butter** or **margarine,** at room temperature
- ¾ cup **granulated sugar**
- 2 ounces **almond paste,** crumbled or shredded (about ⅓ cup)
- ½ cup **all-purpose flour**
  Powdered sugar and **Chocolate Walls** (page 43), optional; or **Chocolate Glaze** (recipe follows)

Dissolve coffee in hot water. Stir in chocolate. In large bowl of an electric mixer, beat egg whites on high speed until they hold stiff, moist peaks.

In another bowl, beat butter and granulated sugar until creamy. Beat in almond paste; mix in egg yolks, chocolate mixture, and flour. Fold in egg whites, about ⅓ at a time, just until blended. Spread batter in a greased, cocoa-dusted 8-inch round cake pan and bake in a 350° oven until cake springs back when lightly touched (about 30 minutes; do not overbake).

Let cool in pan on a rack for about 10 minutes, then invert from pan onto a small tray or a plate. Let cool completely. Wrap airtight; store in refrigerator for up to 2 days, in freezer for up to 1 month.

If desired, apply Chocolate Walls to sides of cake as directed. Refrigerate cake until ready to give. Just before giving, set a paper doily on cake; sift powdered sugar over cake, then carefully lift off doily. Or prepare glaze, if desired; spread over top and sides of cake. Let stand until glaze is hardened (2 to 4 hours) or refrigerate for 10 to 15 minutes. On gift tag, note that cake should be served at room temperature. Makes 1 (8-inch) cake.

CHOCOLATE GLAZE. In the top of a double boiler over barely simmering water, stir 4 ounces **semisweet chocolate** (coarsely chopped) and 1 tablespoon **solid vegetable shortening** just until melted. Remove from heat. Let cool, stirring occasionally, until slightly thickened; then use.

While still warm from the oven, these gift-size
Liqueur Pound Cakes (facing page) are doused with a simple syrup flavored
with rum or sweet liqueur. As the syrup soaks in,
it flavors the cakes—and helps keep them moist and fresh-tasting for days.

PERSIMMON PUDDING

Preparation time: 35 to 40 minutes
Steaming time: 2¼ hours for large mold; 1½ hours for small molds
Storage time: Up to 2 weeks in refrigerator, up to 1 month in freezer for pudding; up to 3 days in refrigerator for sauce

This luscious steamed pudding features a generous helping of puréed soft persimmons. Along with the pudding, include our tangy Lemon Sauce (or perhaps a jar of purchased hard sauce).

> 1½ cups *each* sugar and all-purpose flour
> 1½ teaspoons ground cinnamon
> ½ teaspoon ground nutmeg
> 1 tablespoon baking soda
> 3 tablespoons hot water
> 1½ cups ripe persimmon purée
> 2 eggs
> 1½ cups chopped pitted prunes
> 1 cup coarsely chopped almonds, walnuts, hazelnuts, or pistachios
> About ½ cup brandy
> 2 teaspoons vanilla
> 1½ teaspoons lemon juice
> ¾ cup (¼ lb. plus ¼ cup) butter or margarine, melted and cooled
> Lemon Sauce (recipe follows)

In a bowl, mix sugar, flour, cinnamon, and nutmeg. In a large bowl, stir together baking soda and hot water, then beat in persimmon purée and eggs. Blend in flour mixture, prunes, almonds, ⅓ cup of the brandy, vanilla, lemon juice, and butter.

Scrape batter into a buttered plain or tube-shaped 9- to 10-cup pudding mold or two 4- to 5-cup pudding molds. Cover tightly with lid. Place on a rack in a deep 5- to 6-quart (or larger) pan. Add 1 inch of water, cover pan, and steam over medium heat until pudding is firm when lightly pressed in center (about 2¼ hours for large mold; about 1½ hours for small molds). Add boiling water as needed to keep 1 inch in pan.

Uncover pudding(s); let stand on a rack until slightly cooled (about 15 minutes). Invert onto a dish; lift off mold(s); let cool completely. If desired, wrap pudding(s) in a single layer of cheesecloth and moisten with remaining 3 to 4 tablespoons brandy. Wrap airtight; store in refrigerator for up to 2 weeks, in freezer for up to 1 month.

Before giving, discard cheesecloth (if used). Prepare Lemon Sauce; present along with pudding. On gift tag, give reheating instructions for pudding: wrap pudding in foil and steam on a rack over 1 inch of boiling water in a covered 5- to 6-quart pan until hot (30 to 45 minutes). Makes 1 large pudding or 2 small puddings.

LEMON SAUCE. In a small pan, mix 1 cup **sugar,** ½ cup (¼ lb.) **butter** or margarine, and ¼ cup **lemon juice.** Bring to a boil over medium heat, stirring. Beat 1 **egg** with 1 teaspoon grated **lemon peel** and 3 tablespoons **water.** Beat ¼ cup of the hot sugar mixture into egg mixture; then stir back into pan. Cook, stirring, until thickened. Let cool; pour into a container, cover tightly, and store in refrigerator for up to 3 days. On gift tag, note that sauce should be served hot. Makes about 1½ cups.

PANFORTINAS

Preparation time: 45 to 55 minutes
Baking time: 30 to 35 minutes
Storage time: Up to 2 months at room temperature

To bake these charming miniature versions of the fruitcake-like Italian confection called *panforte,* you'll need to collect a few empty cans (the size used for water chestnuts or tuna). For giving, wrap the cakes in plastic wrap and tie with bright ribbons.

> 2½ to 3 tablespoons butter or margarine, at room temperature
> All-purpose flour
> 2 cups (⅔ lb.) whole blanched almonds
> 1 cup candied orange peel, coarsely chopped
> 1 cup candied lemon peel, minced
> 1 teaspoon *each* grated orange peel and ground cinnamon
> ½ teaspoon ground ginger
> ¼ teaspoon *each* ground allspice and nutmeg
> ½ cup all-purpose flour
> ¾ cup *each* granulated sugar and honey
> 2 tablespoons butter or margarine
> Powdered sugar

Remove both ends from 6 cans, each about 3 inches in diameter and 1½ inches tall. Wash and dry cans. Measure circumference and height of each can, then cut parchment paper strips to fit against sides.

Lightly butter both sides of paper strips. Heavily butter cans' inner sides and press paper strips around sides so they stick. Lightly butter a 12- by 15-inch baking sheet and line with parchment paper. Butter paper and lightly dust with flour. (To butter paper, cans, and baking sheet, you will need 2½ to 3 tablespoons butter *total.*) Set paper-lined cans slightly apart on baking sheet.

Spread almonds in a shallow baking pan and toast in a 350° oven until golden (about 8 minutes), shaking pan frequently. In a large bowl, combine almonds, candied orange peel, lemon peel, grated orange peel, cinnamon, ginger, allspice, nutmeg, and the ½ cup flour; mix to coat fruit with flour.

In a deep 3- to 4-quart pan, combine granulated sugar, honey, and the 2 tablespoons butter. Cook over high heat, stirring, until syrup reaches 265°F on a candy thermometer. Pour hot syrup into nut mixture and blend thoroughly. Spoon into prepared cans, filling them about half full.

Bake in a 300° oven until tops of cakes are lightly browned all over (30 to 35 minutes). Let cool completely. With a wide spatula, scrape panfortinas free from baking sheet. Cut around bottom edge of each can, if needed, to release; then gently push out panfortina. Peel off paper and generously coat cake with powdered sugar. Wrap airtight and store at room temperature for up to 2 months. On gift tag, suggest cutting cakes into small wedges to serve. Makes 6 panfortinas.

APPLESAUCE FRUITCAKE

Preparation time: About 25 minutes
Baking time: About 1¾ hours
Storage time: Up to 1 week at room temperature; up to 1 month in freezer

Want to send someone a birthday party? Here's the cake—a moist, spicy, fruit-filled loaf that keeps and travels beautifully. Pack it in a box, then add candles, party favors, balloons, or anything else you like. (See the photo on page 47 for ideas.)

- ¾ cup (¼ lb. plus ¼ cup) butter or margarine, at room temperature
- 2 cups sugar
- 3 eggs
- 1 teaspoon grated lemon peel
- 1½ cups (about one 14-oz. jar) applesauce
- 3 cups all-purpose flour
- ½ teaspoon salt
- ¾ teaspoon *each* baking soda and ground cloves
- 1½ teaspoons *each* baking powder and ground cinnamon
- 1 cup snipped dried apricots
- 2 tablespoons water or apple juice
- 1½ cups snipped pitted dates
- 1 cup *each* raisins and chopped walnuts

In large bowl of an electric mixer, beat butter and sugar until well blended. Add eggs, 1 at a time, beating well after each addition. Blend in lemon

peel and applesauce. Set aside. In another bowl, stir together 2½ cups of the flour, salt, baking soda, cloves, baking powder, and cinnamon; set aside. In a third bowl, combine apricots and water; let stand for 5 minutes, then mix in dates, raisins, walnuts, and remaining ½ cup flour.

Stir flour-spice mixture into creamed mixture; then add fruit mixture and stir until well blended. Pour batter evenly into 2 greased, flour-dusted 5- by 9-inch loaf pans. Bake in a 325° oven until a wooden pick inserted in center of cake comes out clean (about 1¾ hours). Let cool completely in pans on a rack. Then remove from pans, wrap airtight, and store at room temperature for up to 1 week, in freezer for up to 1 month. Makes 2 cakes.

WESTERN FRUITCAKE

♥ ♥ ♥

Preparation time: 25 to 30 minutes
Baking time: About 1½ hours
Storage time: Up to 2 months in refrigerator

A delightful choice for Christmas giving, this colorful cake features dried apricots, raisins, and dates instead of the traditional candied fruits.

- Butter or margarine, at room temperature
- 1 package (8 oz.) pitted dates, quartered
- 2 cups quartered dried apricots
- 1 cup *each* golden raisins, whole blanched almonds, walnut pieces, and candied cherries
- ¾ cup *each* all-purpose flour and sugar
- ½ teaspoon baking powder
- 3 eggs
- 1 teaspoon vanilla
- Rum or brandy (optional)

Butter a 5- by 9-inch loaf pan; line with parchment or wax paper, then butter paper. Set pan aside.

In a large bowl, combine dates, apricots, raisins, almonds, walnuts, and cherries. In another bowl, stir together flour, sugar, and baking powder; add to fruit mixture and mix evenly.

Beat together eggs and vanilla. Stir thoroughly into fruit mixture. Spoon batter into prepared pan and spread evenly; press batter into corners of pan.

Bake in a 300° oven until golden brown (about 1½ hours). Let cool in pan on a rack for 10 minutes, then turn out of pan. Peel off paper and let cake cool completely on rack.

Wrap airtight; store in refrigerator for at least 2 days or up to 2 months before giving. If desired, sprinkle top of cake with 1 tablespoon rum or brandy once a week. Makes 1 cake.

To show Mom how much you care, present her with an elegant dessert
on Mother's Day—Almond Fudge Cake (page 38), with dark chocolate "walls" and
powdered sugar on top; Nut-crusted Almond Cake
(facing page); or French Almond Cake (facing page), cloaked in marzipan and bedecked
with chocolate ribbons.

FRENCH ALMOND CAKE

(Pictured on facing page)

Preparation time: 1¼ to 1½ hours
Baking time: 30 to 35 minutes
Storage time: Up to 1 day at room temperature

Here's the perfect gift for a connoisseur with a sweet tooth: a firm, fine-textured almond cake filled with raspberry jam and wrapped in a cloak of smooth white marzipan. A tangle of dark chocolate "ribbons" makes an elegant garnish. Another time, you might wrap the cake in chocolate "walls" or try our almond-crusted, lemon-glazed variation.

14	to 16 ounces (about 1½ cups) **marzipan** or **almond paste**
3	**eggs**
2	teaspoons **kirsch, orange-flavored liqueur,** or **vanilla**
2	tablespoons *each* **all-purpose flour** and **cornstarch**
3	tablespoons **butter** or margarine, melted and cooled
	Egg white (if needed)
	Powdered sugar
⅓	cup **raspberry jam**
	Chocolate Ribbons (recipe follows)

Crumble 7 to 8 ounces of the marzipan into large bowl of an electric mixer. Add eggs, 1 at a time, beating until blended. Then beat on high speed until thick, light, and about doubled in volume (about 15 minutes). Beat in kirsch. Sift flour and cornstarch over batter; gently fold in. Pour melted butter over batter; gently fold until blended. Pour into a buttered 8-inch round cake pan.

Bake in a 325° oven until cake just begins to pull from pan sides and feels firm when lightly pressed in center (30 to 35 minutes). Let cool in pan on a rack for 10 minutes, then invert onto rack and let cool completely.

Form remaining 7 to 8 ounces marzipan (or almond paste) into a flat, round patty. (If almond paste is stiff and heavy, knead until smooth with 1 tablespoon egg white and ⅓ cup powdered sugar; if sticky, add more powdered sugar.) Lay marzipan patty on a sheet of wax paper lightly sprinkled with powdered sugar. Sprinkle marzipan lightly with powdered sugar and cover with another sheet of wax paper. Roll out to form an 11-inch circle.

Split cooled cake layer in half horizontally to make 2 layers. Place 1 layer, cut side up, on a flat surface. Spread with jam. Set remaining layer, cut side down, on top. Peel off top sheet of paper from marzipan. Center marzipan over cake, then flop it onto cake; peel off other sheet of paper. Press marzipan gently against sides of cake, pleating edges; evenly trim bottom edge. Using a wide spatula, gently transfer cake to a plate or tray. Wrap airtight; store at room temperature for up to 1 day.

Before giving, decorate cake with Chocolate Ribbons. Makes 1 (8-inch) cake.

CHOCOLATE RIBBONS. In the top of a double boiler over barely simmering water, stir together ½ cup **semisweet chocolate chips,** 1½ teaspoons **light corn syrup,** and 1½ teaspoons **butter** or margarine until chocolate is melted (mixture may look grainy).

Pour mixture onto a 15-inch-long sheet of wax paper. Top with a second sheet of wax paper, then roll out to a layer about ⅛ inch thick. Slide paper onto a baking sheet; refrigerate until chocolate is firm (about 20 minutes).

Peel off top paper; let chocolate stand at room temperature until slightly soft (about 5 minutes). Then, with a sharp knife, cut just through chocolate—not paper—to make ¼-inch-wide "ribbons." Peel off one by one and drape as many as you like atop cake.

CHOCOLATE WALLS. Prepare chocolate mixture as for **Chocolate Ribbons;** roll out between sheets of wax paper and refrigerate as directed.

Measure height and circumference of cake. Peel off top paper from chocolate; cut through chocolate and bottom paper to make a strip as wide as cake is tall and about 3 inches longer than cake's circumference. Wrap chocolate strip around cake. Peel off paper; trim overlap, then press to adhere. (If necessary, cut 2 shorter strips and apply to cake. To join strips, overlap ends; dip knife blade in hot water, dry, and use to smooth seams.)

NUT-CRUSTED ALMOND CAKE

(Pictured on facing page)

Generously butter bottom and sides of an 8-inch round cake pan. Press ½ cup **sliced almonds** evenly over pan bottom and sides. Prepare batter for **French Almond Cake;** carefully pour into pan. Bake as directed. Let cool in pan on a rack for 10 minutes. Holding rack over pan, flip to release cake; invert to put cake back in pan, nut side down.

Pierce warm cake with a wooden pick, spacing holes ½ inch apart. Blend 2 tablespoons **lemon juice** and ½ cup **powdered sugar;** pour over cake. Let cake cool completely in pan, then invert (nut side up) and wrap airtight. Store at room temperature for up to 1 day, in freezer for up to 1 month.

HAMANTASHEN

♥ ♥ ♥

Preparation time: About 50 minutes, plus 3 hours to chill dough
Baking time: About 15 minutes
Storage time: Up to 3 days at room temperature; up to 1 month in freezer

These triangular fruit-filled cookies are traditional during Purim—the Jewish holiday in early March that commemorates the thwarting of a Persian plot against the Jews. Hamantashen take their name and shape from the tricornered hat worn by Haman, a chief minister of the Persians.

 ½ **cup sugar**
 ½ **cup (¼ lb.) butter or margarine,**
  at room temperature
 ¼ **cup honey**
 1 **teaspoon *each* vanilla and vinegar**
 2 **eggs**
 1½ **cups *each* whole wheat flour and**
  all-purpose flour
 2 **teaspoons baking powder**
 1 **teaspoon ground cinnamon**
 ½ **teaspoon baking soda**
  Raisin–Poppy Seed Filling or
  Apricot Filling (recipes follow)

In large bowl of an electric mixer, beat sugar, butter, honey, vanilla, vinegar, and eggs until blended.

 In a small bowl, stir together whole wheat flour, all-purpose flour, baking powder, cinnamon, and baking soda. Add to creamed mixture and stir to blend. Cover tightly with plastic wrap and refrigerate for at least 3 hours or until next day. Meanwhile, prepare filling of your choice and set aside.

 On a floured board, roll out dough to a thickness of ⅛ inch. Cut out with a 3-inch round cookie cutter. Set cookies slightly apart on lightly greased baking sheets. Spoon a generous teaspoon of filling onto center of each. Bring edges up to form a triangle; pinch seams together to seal. Bake in a 350° oven until edges are browned (about 15 minutes). Transfer to racks and let cool completely. Wrap airtight; store at room temperature for up to 3 days, in freezer for up to 1 month. Makes about 2 dozen cookies.

RAISIN–POPPY SEED FILLING. In a small bowl, mix 5 tablespoons **poppy seeds,** ¾ cup **raisins,** 2 tablespoons **honey,** 2 tablespoons **butter** or margarine (melted), and 2 teaspoons grated **lemon peel.**

APRICOT FILLING. In a small bowl, mix ½ cup finely chopped **dried apricots,** ½ cup finely chopped **almonds** or walnuts, 2 tablespoons **honey,** 2 tablespoons **butter** or margarine (melted), and ¼ teaspoon **ground cinnamon** or ground ginger.

FUDGE BROWNIES

♥ ♥ ♥

Preparation time: About 20 minutes
Baking time: About 35 minutes
Storage time: 2 to 3 days at room temperature; up to 1 month in freezer

A perennial favorite, these fudgy little squares are ideal for mailing: thanks to their soft texture and sturdy shape, they won't break or crumble.

 ½ **cup (¼ lb.) butter or margarine**
 4 **ounces unsweetened chocolate**
 2 **cups sugar**
 1½ **teaspoons vanilla**
 4 **eggs**
 1 **cup all-purpose flour**
 ½ **to 1 cup coarsely chopped walnuts**

In a 2- to 3-quart pan, melt butter and chocolate over medium-low heat, stirring until well blended. Remove from heat and stir in sugar and vanilla. Add eggs, 1 at a time, beating well after each addition. Stir in flour; then mix in walnuts.

 Spread batter evenly in a greased 9-inch square baking pan. Bake in a 325° oven until brownie feels dry on top (about 35 minutes). Let cool completely in pan on a rack, then cut into 2¼-inch squares. Remove from pan and wrap airtight; store at room temperature for 2 to 3 days, in freezer for up to 1 month. Makes 16 brownies.

CHOCOLATE CHIP COOKIES AT THEIR BEST

♥ ♥ ♥

Preparation time: About 25 minutes
Baking time: 16 to 19 minutes
Storage time: 2 to 3 days at room temperature; up to 1 month in freezer

There's nothing modest about these cookies— they're impressively big and chock-full of chocolate and nuts. Mix them with an equal number of their white chocolate cousins (recipe follows), and you've got a gift that's a sure winner.

1 cup (½ lb.) butter or margarine,
   at room temperature
½ cup solid vegetable shortening
1⅓ cups granulated sugar
1 cup firmly packed brown sugar
4 eggs
1 tablespoon vanilla
1 teaspoon lemon juice
3 cups all-purpose flour
2 teaspoons baking soda
1½ teaspoons salt
1 teaspoon ground cinnamon (optional)
½ cup rolled oats
2 large packages (12 oz. *each*) semisweet
   chocolate chips
2 cups chopped walnuts

In large bowl of an electric mixer, beat butter, short-ening, granulated sugar, and brown sugar on high speed until very light and fluffy (about 5 minutes). Add eggs, 1 at a time, beating well after each addi-tion. Beat in vanilla and lemon juice. In another bowl, stir together flour, baking soda, salt, cinna-mon (if used), and oats. Gradually add to butter mixture, blending thoroughly. Stir in chocolate chips and walnuts.

Use a scant ¼ cup of dough for each cookie. Drop dough onto lightly greased baking sheets, spacing cookies 3 to 4 inches apart. For soft cook-ies, bake in a 325° oven until light golden brown (17 to 19 minutes); for crisp cookies, bake in a 350° oven until golden brown (16 to 18 minutes). Transfer to racks and let cool completely. Wrap airtight and store at room temperature for 2 to 3 days, in freezer for up to 1 month. Makes about 3 dozen cookies.

WHITE CHOCOLATE CHIP COOKIES

Preparation time: About 25 minutes
Baking time: 12 to 14 minutes
Storage time: 2 to 3 days at room temperature; up to 1 month in freezer

What could be better than a chocolate chip cookie? To some ways of thinking, this white chocolate chip version is a delectable improvement on tradition.

1 cup (½ lb.) butter or margarine,
   at room temperature
1½ cups sugar
2 teaspoons baking soda
1 egg

1 cup plus 2 tablespoons all-purpose flour
2 cups quick-cooking rolled oats
6 ounces white chocolate, coarsely
   chopped (1¼ cups)

In large bowl of an electric mixer, beat butter, sugar, and baking soda until creamy; beat in egg. Gradu-ally add flour and oats, blending thoroughly. Stir in chocolate.

Roll 2-tablespoon portions of dough into balls and place 4 inches apart on greased baking sheets. Bake in a 350° oven until light golden brown (12 to 14 minutes). Let cool on baking sheets until firm to the touch, then transfer to racks and let cool com-pletely. Wrap airtight; store at room temperature for 2 to 3 days, in freezer for up to 1 month. Makes about 2½ dozen cookies.

OATMEAL RAISIN COOKIES

Preparation time: About 20 minutes
Baking time: About 15 minutes
*Storage time: Up to 3 days at room temperature;
up to 1 month in freezer*

A good candidate for mailing, these plump, chewy cookies are an ever-popular choice for snacking. In this version, they're delightfully pebbled with oats, raisins, and nuts.

1 cup (½ lb.) butter or margarine,
   at room temperature
2 cups firmly packed brown sugar
2 eggs
3 tablespoons lemon juice
2 cups all-purpose flour
1 teaspoon *each* salt and baking soda
3 cups quick-cooking rolled oats
1½ cups raisins
1 cup chopped walnuts

In large bowl of an electric mixer, beat butter and sugar until creamy; then beat in eggs and lemon juice. In another bowl, stir together flour, salt, and baking soda; gradually add to butter mixture, blending thoroughly. Add oats, raisins, and walnuts; stir until well combined.

Drop dough by rounded tablespoonfuls onto ungreased baking sheets, spacing cookies about 2 inches apart. Bake in a 350° oven until edges of cookies are golden brown (about 15 minutes). Transfer to racks and let cool completely. Wrap air-tight; store at room temperature for up to 3 days, in freezer for up to 1 month. Makes about 4 dozen cookies.

Nürnberger Lebkuchen

♥ ♥ ♥

Preparation time: About 1 hour, plus 8 hours to chill dough
Baking time: 12 to 15 minutes
Storage time: Up to 3 months at room temperature

A Christmas tradition from Germany, these spicy, cakelike honey cookies are perfect make-aheads for holiday giving. In fact, they *must* age for at least several weeks to become soft and chewy.

- 1 cup honey
- ¾ cup firmly packed dark brown sugar
- 1 egg, lightly beaten
- 1 tablespoon lemon juice
- 1 teaspoon grated lemon peel
- 2⅓ cups all-purpose flour
- 1 teaspoon ground cinnamon
- ½ teaspoon *each* ground allspice, cloves, and nutmeg
- ½ teaspoon *each* salt and baking soda
- ⅓ cup *each* finely chopped candied citron and finely chopped almonds
- About 24 candied cherries, cut in half
- 6 to 8 ounces whole blanched almonds
- Rum Glaze (recipe follows)

Heat honey in a small pan over medium-high heat just until it begins to bubble. Remove from heat and let cool slightly. Stir in sugar, egg, lemon juice, and lemon peel; let cool to lukewarm.

In a large bowl, stir together flour, cinnamon, allspice, cloves, nutmeg, salt, and baking soda. Add honey mixture, citron, and chopped almonds; stir until well blended (dough will be soft). Cover tightly with plastic wrap and refrigerate for at least 8 hours or for up to 2 days.

Work with ¼ of the dough at a time, keeping remaining dough refrigerated. On a heavily floured board, roll out dough with a floured rolling pin to a thickness of ⅜ inch. Cut dough with a 2½-inch round cookie cutter; place cookies 2 inches apart on baking sheets lined with lightly greased parchment paper.

Press a cherry half into center of each cookie; surround with 3 almonds arranged like flower petals. Bake in a 375° oven until golden brown (12 to 15 minutes). Meanwhile, prepare Rum Glaze. Remove cookies from oven and immediately brush glaze over tops with a pastry brush; transfer to racks and let cool. As soon as top glaze dries, turn cookies over and brush glaze over bottoms.

Let cookies stand until completely cool and dry, then pack into airtight containers and store at room temperature for at least 2 weeks or for up to 3 months before giving. If cookies get slightly hard, add a thin slice of apple to each container; cover tightly and store until cookies are moist again (about 1 day), then discard apple. Makes about 4 dozen cookies.

Rum Glaze. Stir together 1 cup **powdered sugar** and 5 tablespoons **rum** until smooth.

Cheesecake Squares

♥ ♥ ♥

Preparation time: About 25 minutes
Baking time: About 35 minutes
Storage time: Up to 3 days in refrigerator

With their creamy filling and nut-crunchy crust, these luscious bars are a welcome contribution to a potluck—and an enticing treat for friends—at any time of year.

- ⅓ cup butter or margarine, at room temperature
- ⅓ cup firmly packed brown sugar
- 1 cup all-purpose flour
- ½ cup finely chopped walnuts
- ¼ cup granulated sugar
- 1 large package (8 oz.) cream cheese, at room temperature
- 1 egg
- ½ teaspoon vanilla
- 2 tablespoons milk
- 1 tablespoon lemon juice

In large bowl of an electric mixer, beat butter and brown sugar until creamy. With a fork, blend in flour until mixture resembles fine crumbs. Stir in walnuts. Reserve 1 cup of the crumb mixture for topping; press remainder firmly and evenly over bottom of a greased 8-inch square baking pan. Bake in a 350° oven until lightly browned (12 to 15 minutes).

Meanwhile, in small bowl of mixer, beat granulated sugar and cream cheese until fluffy. Add egg, vanilla, milk, and lemon juice; beat until smooth. Pour cream cheese mixture over baked crust; sprinkle evenly with reserved crumb mixture.

Return to oven and bake until top is lightly browned (about 20 more minutes). Let cool completely in pan on a rack, then cut into 2-inch squares. Remove from pan, wrap airtight, and store in refrigerator for up to 3 days. Makes 16 bars.

Cake, candles, gifts, and all! A party in a box will delight a friend
of any age who's spending a birthday away from home. Choose a cake that keeps
well, like our Applesauce Fruitcake (page 41), Lemon Loaf Cake
(page 37), or Liqueur Pound Cake (page 38)—or use a purchased unfrosted cake, if you
prefer. Pack the celebration in a sturdy box with plenty of packing material.

PEPPERMINT SLICES

Preparation time: About 15 minutes, plus 2 hours to chill dough
Baking time: About 8 minutes
Storage time: Up to 4 days at room temperature;
up to 1 month in freezer

Tinted pastel pink or green, these crisp, minty morsels are perfect for Easter or Christmas. Each cookie sports a sparkling edging of colored decorating sugar.

- 2 **cups (1 lb.) butter, at room temperature**
- 1 **cup powdered sugar**
- 1 **teaspoon mint extract**
  Red or green food color
  Pinch of salt
- 2½ **cups all-purpose flour**
  Red or green decorating sugar

In large bowl of an electric mixer, beat butter and powdered sugar until fluffy; beat in mint extract and enough food color to tint mixture pink or green. Mix in salt and flour. Shape dough into rolls about 2 inches in diameter. Spread decorating sugar on a sheet of wax paper; set rolls in sugar and turn to coat evenly. Then wrap each roll in wax paper and refrigerate until firm (about 2 hours) or for up to 3 days.

Unwrap dough. Using a sharp knife, cut dough into ⅛-inch-thick slices; place slices 1 inch apart on ungreased baking sheets. Bake in a 375° oven until very lightly browned around edges (about 8 minutes). Transfer to racks and let cool completely. Wrap airtight; store at room temperature for up to 4 days, in freezer for up to 1 month. Makes about 6 dozen cookies.

RASPBERRY-NUT VALENTINES

Preparation time: 45 to 55 minutes, plus 1 to 2 hours to chill dough
Baking time: 8 to 10 minutes
Storage time: 1 to 2 days at room temperature

Fancy enough for high tea, sweet and pretty enough for a Valentine offering, these rich, European-style nut cookies have a luscious jam filling.

- 1⅓ **cups pecans**
- 1 **cup (½ lb.) butter or margarine,**
  at room temperature
- ⅔ **cup granulated sugar**

- ½ **teaspoon vanilla**
- 2 **cups all-purpose flour**
  Powdered sugar
  About ¼ cup raspberry jam

In a blender or food processor, whirl pecans until finely ground. Set aside. In large bowl of an electric mixer, beat butter and granulated sugar until creamy; beat in vanilla. Gradually add pecans and flour, blending thoroughly. Cover tightly with plastic wrap and refrigerate until easy to handle (1 to 2 hours) or for up to 3 days.

On a floured board, roll out dough to a thickness of ⅛ inch. Cut out with a 2-inch heart-shaped cookie cutter and transfer to ungreased baking sheets, spacing about 1 inch apart. Cut a hole in center of half of the cookies, using a tiny cutter about ½ inch in diameter. Bake in a 375° oven until lightly browned (8 to 10 minutes). Transfer to racks and let cool completely.

Sift powdered sugar over tops of cookies with holes; then spread bottom sides of remaining cookies with jam. Place a sugar-topped cookie on each jam-topped cookie to form a sandwich. Wrap airtight; store at room temperature for 1 to 2 days. Makes about 3 dozen cookies.

THUMBPRINT COOKIES

(Pictured on front cover)

Preparation time: About 25 minutes
Baking time: 12 to 15 minutes
Storage time: 2 to 3 days at room temperature; up to 1 month in freezer
(for unfilled cookies)

A sweet "jewel" of jelly sparkles in the center of each of these nutty drop cookies. The bright color makes them an attractive addition to a gift tin of assorted cookies—for Christmas, Valentine's Day, or any occasion.

- 1 **cup (½ lb.) butter or margarine,**
  at room temperature
- ½ **cup firmly packed brown sugar**
- 2 **eggs, separated**
- ½ **teaspoon vanilla**
- 2½ **cups all-purpose flour**
- ¼ **teaspoon salt**
- 1½ **cups finely chopped walnuts**
- 3 **to 4 tablespoons red currant jelly or**
  raspberry jam (or other jelly or jam of
  your choice)

In large bowl of an electric mixer, beat butter and sugar until creamy. Beat in egg yolks and vanilla.

In another bowl, stir together flour and salt. Gradually add to butter mixture, blending thoroughly.

In a small bowl, lightly beat egg whites. With your hands, roll dough into balls about 1 inch in diameter. Dip each ball in egg whites, then roll in walnuts to coat. Place 1 inch apart on greased baking sheets.

With your thumb or the tip of a spoon, make an indentation in center of each ball. Bake in a 375° oven until lightly browned (12 to 15 minutes). Let cool on baking sheets for about a minute, then transfer to racks. If necessary, press each indentation again to deepen slightly. Let cookies cool completely. (At this point, you may wrap airtight and freeze for up to 1 month.) Neatly fill each indentation with about ¼ teaspoon jelly. Wrap airtight; store at room temperature for 2 to 3 days. Makes about 3½ dozen cookies.

COCONUT BUTTER COOKIES

(Pictured on front cover)

♥ ♥ ♥

Preparation time: 30 to 45 minutes, plus 2 hours to chill dough
Baking time: About 20 minutes
Storage time: Up to 3 days at room temperature;
up to 1 month in freezer

Icebox cookies are a delicious and practical gift choice; you can make the dough ahead, then simply slice off and bake a chosen number of cookies fresh, when you need them. Coconut adds a sweet, nutty accent to these buttery shortbreads.

   1 **cup (½ lb.) butter, at room temperature**
   ¼ **cup granulated sugar**
   1 **teaspoon vanilla**
   2 **cups all-purpose flour**
   ¼ **teaspoon salt**
   2 **cups sweetened flaked coconut**
     About 1 cup powdered sugar

In large bowl of an electric mixer, beat butter until creamy; add granulated sugar and beat until smooth. Mix in vanilla. In another bowl, stir together flour and salt; gradually add to butter mixture, blending thoroughly. Add coconut and mix until well combined. Shape dough into a roll about 1½ inches in diameter; wrap in wax paper and refrigerate until firm (at least 2 hours) or for up to 3 days.

Unwrap dough. Using a sharp knife, cut into ¼-inch-thick slices; place slices slightly apart on ungreased baking sheets. Bake in a 300° oven until cookies are firm to the touch and lightly browned on bottoms (about 20 minutes). Transfer to racks and let cool for 5 minutes. Sift half the powdered sugar onto wax paper and transfer cookies to it in a single layer; sift remaining powdered sugar on top to cover cookies lightly. Let cookies cool completely. Wrap airtight; store at room temperature for up to 3 days, in freezer for up to 1 month. Makes about 4 dozen cookies.

BROWN SUGAR SHORTBREADS

(Pictured on page 50)

♥ ♥ ♥

Preparation time: 45 to 60 minutes
Baking time: 25 to 40 minutes
Storage time: 2 to 3 days at room temperature; up to 1 month in freezer

For a really festive gift, bake these cookies in purchased cookie molds like the angel shown on page 50. (Some cookie molds may require seasoning before use; check the manufacturer's instructions.)

   1 **cup (½ lb.) butter or margarine,**
     at room temperature
   1 **cup firmly packed brown sugar**
   1 **teaspoon vanilla**
   2½ **cups all-purpose flour**

In large bowl of an electric mixer, beat butter and sugar until creamy; add vanilla. With a heavy wooden spoon, gradually beat in flour, blending thoroughly. Gather dough into a ball.

For rolled cookies: On a lightly floured board, roll out dough to make a rectangle about ¼ inch thick; trim edges to straighten them, then cut rectangle into 1- by 2-inch rectangles. Place slightly apart on ungreased baking sheets; refrigerate until cold. Bake in a 300° oven until firm to touch (25 to 30 minutes).

For molded cookies: Press dough firmly and evenly into a floured wooden or terracotta mold; invert onto an ungreased baking sheet and tap mold firmly to release cookie. Repeat to shape remaining dough; space cookies 1 inch apart. Refrigerate until cold. Bake in a 275° oven until firm to touch (about 40 minutes).

Cool rolled or molded cookies on baking sheets for 5 minutes. Transfer to racks and let cool completely. Wrap airtight; store at room temperature for 2 to 3 days, in freezer for up to 1 month. Makes 4 to 5 dozen 1- by 2-inch rolled cookies, about 6 to 8 4- by 6-inch molded cookies.

One of the joys of Christmas is baking special cookies
to share with friends. The three holiday standouts shown here are Cookie Canvases
(facing page), iced Gingerbread Cutouts (facing page),
and Brown Sugar Shortbreads (page 49) shaped in terracotta molds.

COOKIE CANVASES

(Pictured on facing page)

Preparation time: About 45 minutes, plus 8 hours for glaze to dry
Baking time: 25 to 30 minutes
Storage time: 1 to 2 days at room temperature

If you're artistically inclined, here's your chance to paint a special canvas for everyone on your gift list. You'll need to bake these cookies ahead of time, since they're coated with a glaze that must dry for 8 to 24 hours. Use undiluted food colors, poured into small cups, for paints; apply with watercolor brushes. To prevent colors from bleeding together, let each color dry briefly before painting another over it.

- 2 cups (1 lb.) butter or margarine, at room temperature
- 2 cups granulated sugar
- 2 teaspoons vanilla
- 5 cups all-purpose flour
- 1 to 1½ pounds powdered sugar
- 6 to 9 tablespoons warm water
- Assorted food colors

In large bowl of an electric mixer, beat butter, granulated sugar, and vanilla until creamy. Beat in flour until thoroughly combined. With a floured, stockinet-covered rolling pin, roll out enough dough on an ungreased, unrimmed baking sheet to cover sheet in a ¼- to ⅜-inch-thick layer. Use a sharp knife and a ruler to cut away a 1-inch strip of dough on all sides of baking sheet; make no other cuts.

Combine trimmings with remaining dough; then repeat rolling and cutting until all dough is used. Bake in a 300° oven until cookies are pale gold and centers are firm to the touch (25 to 30 minutes).

Meanwhile, place powdered sugar in a large bowl. Gradually add warm water (about 6 tablespoons per pound), beating constantly, until glaze is smooth and thick; mixture should flow smoothly but set quickly.

Remove cookies from oven. At once, cut into 4- by 6-inch rectangles, using a sharp knife and a ruler; trim to straighten edges. Let cookies cool on baking sheets until just warm to the touch (about 7 minutes).

With a wide spatula, transfer cookies to a flat foil-covered surface. Quickly spread each cookie with enough glaze to make a very smooth surface. Do not cover or move cookies until glaze is dry to the touch (8 to 24 hours).

Paint with food colors. Give right away; or wrap airtight and store at room temperature for 1 to 2 days. Makes about 1 dozen large cookies.

GINGERBREAD CUTOUTS

(Pictured on facing page)

Preparation time: About 1¼ hours, plus 2 hours to chill dough
Baking time: 10 to 15 minutes
Storage time: 1 to 2 days at room temperature; up to 1 month in freezer

Cut out these holiday classics in any shape your fancy dictates, then spruce them up with white icing designs piped on with a pastry bag.

- ½ cup (¼ lb.) butter or margarine, at room temperature
- 1 cup firmly packed brown sugar
- 1½ cups light molasses
- ⅔ cup water or apple juice
- 7 cups all-purpose flour
- 2 teaspoons *each* baking soda and salt
- 1 teaspoon *each* ground cinnamon, ginger, cloves, and allspice
- Royal Icing (recipe follows) or purchased decorating icing

In large bowl of an electric mixer, beat butter and sugar until creamy. Add molasses and beat until blended, then mix in water. In another bowl, stir together flour, baking soda, salt, cinnamon, ginger, cloves, and allspice. Gradually add to butter mixture, blending to form a stiff dough. Cover tightly with plastic wrap and refrigerate for at least 2 hours or until next day.

On a floured board, roll out dough, a portion at a time, to a thickness of ⅛ to ¼ inch. Cut out with a 3- to 3½-inch cookie cutter and, with cutter still in place, transfer cookie and cutter with a wide spatula to a lightly greased baking sheet. Lift off cutter and repeat; leave 2 inches between cookies.

Bake in a 350° oven until lightly browned (10 to 15 minutes). Transfer cookies to racks and let cool completely. Prepare Royal Icing; press icing through a pastry tube with a small tip to add edging and other designs to cookies. Wrap airtight; store at room temperature for 1 to 2 days, in freezer for up to 1 month. Makes 4 to 5 dozen cookies.

ROYAL ICING. In small bowl of an electric mixer, beat 1 **egg white** with ⅛ teaspoon **cream of tartar** and a dash of **salt** for 1 minute on high speed. Add 2 cups **powdered sugar** and beat slowly until blended; then beat on high speed until very stiff (3 to 5 minutes).

CANDIES & SWEETS

Irresistible goodies from your own candy kitchen

Make your candy-loving friends' dreams come true with one or more of the luscious treats from this chapter. There's a tempting selection of chocolate delights, from fudge to dark truffles to a distinctive and different chocolate "pâté"; there are canes of raspberry-flavored taffy, plump dried fruits with a creamy marzipan filling, and even crisp, nut-laden caramel corn (it's addictive)! For Valentine's Day, surprise someone special with an edible heart-shaped chocolate box, filled with truffles. For Easter, present pretty white candy eggs.

If you've always thought of candy making as a complicated process, you'll be pleasantly surprised by how easily most of our recipes can be made. Some, like Almond Bark and Caramel Nut Corn, are simple enough for children to prepare; the fancier offerings take a bit more time and precision, but still go together with unexpected ease.

Plain or elaborate, candies lend themselves readily to pretty packaging. Display them row by row in doily-lined boxes or tins, nestle them in individual gold or silver bonbon cups, or just cluster them on a beautiful plate. Most of the candies in this chapter will keep in the refrigerator for at least a week or so, and many are easy to wrap and ship in the mail (see page 80).

Raspberry Taffy Canes

Preparation time: 1½ to 1¾ hours
Storage time: Up to 1 month in refrigerator or freezer

If you're looking for an out-of-the-ordinary gift for the young (or young at heart), try pretty taffy canes with a fresh, natural berry flavor. Making taffy does require speed and dexterity, but it can be lots of fun once you get into the spirit.

- 1 **bag (12 oz.) frozen sweetened raspberries, thawed**
- 2 **cups sugar**
- ½ **cup light corn syrup**
- 2 **tablespoons water**
  Butter or margarine

Purée undrained thawed raspberries in a food processor or blender; rub through a fine wire strainer and discard seeds. Place purée in a small pan and bring to a boil over medium heat; boil until purée is reduced to ½ cup. Set aside.

In a 1½- to 2-quart pan, combine sugar, corn syrup, and water. Stirring constantly, bring mixture to a rolling boil over high heat. Position a candy thermometer in boiling syrup and cook, without stirring, until syrup reaches 310° to 315°F (about 5 minutes). As syrup cooks, wash off spatters of syrup as they accumulate inside pan, using a stiff brush dipped frequently in water (if crystalline bits of sugar are not washed away, taffy may harden before it is pulled).

As soon as syrup reaches 310° to 315°F, add raspberry purée. *If using a metal-mounted thermometer,* use it to mix concentrate thoroughly into bubbly syrup (if thermometer is removed and allowed to cool slightly, it will not respond quickly enough when returned to pan). *If using a glass thermometer,* leave it in pan, but stir syrup with a spoon. Stir constantly until thermometer registers 270°F.

Immediately, pour hot taffy into a well-buttered rimmed 10- by 15-inch baking pan. With a buttered wide spatula, push taffy from one side of pan to the other until it is cool enough to handle quickly, but still hot; butter exposed pan and spatula frequently to reduce sticking.

Coat hands with butter. Working quickly, pull and stretch taffy until it begins to turn opaque and lighter in color, and is stiffer-textured but still malleable. At this point, it should be cool enough for children to handle.

With buttered scissors, cut taffy into 4 equal portions. To keep taffy malleable, put pieces well apart on a freshly buttered pan and hold in a 150° oven for up to 1 hour (taffy will flatten as it rests).

To make canes, pull a portion of taffy at a time until it turns opaque and satiny. Then, pulling and squeezing, shape taffy into a rope that is the thickness you want. You have to work fast; the taffy is easiest to manage if you work in a warm part of the kitchen.

Cut taffy rope into desired lengths with buttered scissors. Leave ropes plain or twist for a textured finish; curve tips to make canes.

Put canes flat in a single layer on buttered pans and refrigerate until hard. Wrap individually, airtight, in plastic wrap or small plastic bags. Refrigerate or freeze for up to 1 month; if kept longer, canes may become crumbly or sticky. Makes about 1½ pounds taffy (about 2 dozen 10-inch canes).

Almond Bark

Preparation time: About 50 minutes, including chilling time
Storage time: Up to 3 weeks in refrigerator

Here's a confection that couldn't be much simpler to make: you just melt white chocolate chips or white candy coating, then stir in toasted almonds.

White chocolate chips are now available at most supermarkets. Look for white candy coating at candy stores; it's also sold in some well-stocked markets.

- 1 **cup whole unblanched almonds**
- 2⅔ **cups white chocolate chips; or 1 pound white candy coating, coarsely chopped**
- 2 **tablespoons solid vegetable shortening (do not use butter or other shortening)**

Spread almonds in a baking pan and toast in a 350° oven just until lightly browned beneath skins (about 8 minutes), shaking pan frequently. Let cool.

Line a rimmed 10- by 15-inch baking pan with wax paper, covering bottom and sides of pan.

Place white chocolate chips and shortening in the top of a double boiler over barely simmering water. Stir just until mixture begins to melt. Remove top of double boiler from water; stir until mixture is completely melted. Stir in almonds.

Turn mixture into pan and spread to distribute nuts evenly; to spread more smoothly, drop pan onto counter several times from a height of about 8 inches. Refrigerate candy just until firm (about 30 minutes). Break into pieces. Wrap airtight and store in refrigerator for up to 3 weeks. Makes about 1¼ pounds candy.

CHOCOLATE VALENTINE BOXES

(Pictured on facing page)

♥ ♥ ♥

Preparation time: About 1½ hours, including cooling and chilling time
Storage time: Up to 2 weeks in refrigerator

To make these professional-looking edible boxes, you simply coat a plastic candy mold (available in craft, cookware, or candy supply stores) or a foil-lined box or pan with melted chocolate or candy coating, then chill and unmold. The finished boxes make delightful containers for Hazelnut Chocolate Truffles (page 56) or other treats.

> 8 **ounces bittersweet or semisweet chocolate, chocolate candy coating, or white candy coating, coarsely chopped (do not use chocolate chips or white chocolate)**

Place chocolate in the top of a double boiler over hot (not simmering) water; stir just until half the chocolate is melted. Remove top of double boiler from water and stir until chocolate is completely melted. Let cool to room temperature, stirring occasionally (30 to 45 minutes).

To make boxes, use heart-shaped, 1-inch-deep plastic molds or foil-lined boxes or pans. The chocolate will make one 10-inch-wide box without lid, one 6-inch-wide box with lid, or two 4-inch-wide boxes with lids (measure molds at widest point). If mold doesn't include a lid, make a pattern. Cover an unrimmed baking sheet with foil and fold foil snugly under sheet. Using mold as a guide, trace a slightly larger heart onto foil.

To make a box, wipe out molds with a clean, soft cloth. Pour all the chocolate into a 10-inch-wide mold (or pour ⅔ of the chocolate into a 6-inch-wide mold, or ⅓ of the chocolate into *each* of two 4-inch-wide molds). Use any remaining chocolate for lids.

Tilt mold to coat bottom and sides with chocolate. If necessary, use back of a spoon to push chocolate up sides (not over rim). Sides of box should be about ⅛ inch thick; if chocolate slides down and makes thinner sides, pour excess chocolate from bottom of box into a bowl and hold at room temperature. Tap mold lightly on counter to release air bubbles. Refrigerate just until chocolate is firm. Scoop any reserved chocolate from bowl onto back of a spoon and spread it on box sides, using all. Refrigerate until firm (about 15 minutes).

To make lids using a plastic mold, pour remaining chocolate (not used for boxes) into lid; use all the remaining chocolate for a 6-inch lid, half the chocolate for *each* 4-inch lid. Tilt molds to coat bottom and sides. Refrigerate until firm (15 minutes).

To make lids using traced outlines, pour all the remaining chocolate into center of a large pattern, or half into *each* of 2 small patterns. With back of a spoon, spread chocolate to edges of outline. Refrigerate until firm (about 15 minutes).

To release boxes and lids from molds, invert molds on a flat surface; tap gently. If needed, peel off foil. If boxes break or are flawed, remelt chocolate and start again. *To release traced lids,* remove foil from baking sheet; peel foil from chocolate.

To store, cover and refrigerate for up to 2 weeks. Makes 1 (10-inch) box without lid, 1 (6-inch) box with lid, or 2 (4-inch) boxes with lids.

To coat mold with chocolate, tilt to cover bottom and sides (left). Refrigerate until firm. To release box, place inverted mold on a flat surface, then gently wiggle and tap (right).

CHOCOLATE PÂTÉ

♥ ♥ ♥

Preparation time: About 10 minutes
Storage time: Up to 6 weeks in refrigerator

Soft, spoonable, and intensely flavored, this luxurious chocolate "pâté" is a versatile gift. The lucky recipient can eat it as a simple dessert along with pound cake, cookies, or fruit, or warm it to pour over ice cream (just set the container in a bowl of hot water and stir until the pâté is pourable).

> 1 **pound semisweet chocolate, finely chopped, or 2⅔ cups semisweet chocolate chips**
> 6 **tablespoons butter or margarine, cut into small pieces**
> ¾ **cup whipping cream**

Put chocolate and butter in a large bowl and nest over hot water (not on heat). In a small pan, bring cream to a boil; pour over chocolate. Stir until chocolate and butter are melted and smoothly blended. Pour into several small containers or 1 larger (3-cup) container. Let cool, then cover airtight and store in refrigerator for up to 6 weeks. Makes 2⅔ cups.

Professional-looking boxes of dark or white chocolate
(facing page) are sure to make a big impression on your valentine. To create them,
you simply spread melted chocolate in heart-shaped
plastic candy molds or pans and chill until firm. Fill the delectable boxes with rich
Hazelnut Chocolate Truffles (page 56).

CHOCOLATE CREME FUDGE

Preparation time: 45 to 60 minutes, including chilling time
Storage time: Up to 2 weeks in refrigerator

Almost anyone with a sweet tooth likes fudge! This version is just about foolproof; it's made by a simplified method using marshmallow creme.

  1 **small can (5 oz.) evaporated milk**
  1⅓ **cups sugar**
  ¼ **teaspoon salt**
  ¼ **cup butter or margarine**
  1 **small package (6 oz.) semisweet chocolate chips**
  ¾ **cup or ½ jar (7-oz. size) marshmallow creme**
  1 **teaspoon vanilla**
  ½ **cup chopped walnuts or pecans**

In a 2½- to 3-quart pan, combine evaporated milk, sugar, salt, and butter. Bring to a rolling boil over medium-low heat, stirring; cook, stirring, for 5 minutes. (If heat is too high, mixture will scorch.)

Remove from heat; add chocolate chips and stir until melted. Quickly stir in marshmallow creme, vanilla, and walnuts until blended. Pour into a buttered 8-inch square baking pan; spread to make an even layer. Let cool, then cover and refrigerate until firm (30 to 45 minutes). Cut into 1-inch squares, wrap airtight, and store in refrigerator for up to 2 weeks. Makes 2 pounds (about 5 dozen pieces).

NUT-TOPPED TOFFEE

Preparation time: About 45 minutes, including chilling time
Storage time: Up to 3 days in a cool place (below 75°F)

Crunchy nuts and chocolate candy bars make the topping for this buttery-tasting toffee. Package the crisp morsels in tins, boxes, or glass canisters.

  1 **cup (½ lb.) butter (do not use margarine)**
  1 **cup firmly packed brown sugar**
  6 **bars (1⅜ oz. *each*) milk chocolate**
  ½ **cup finely chopped hazelnuts or almonds**

In a deep pan, combine butter and sugar. Cook over medium-high heat, stirring constantly, until mixture reaches 300°F (hard crack stage) on a candy thermometer. Pour immediately into a buttered 9-inch square baking pan. Lay chocolate bars over hot candy and let stand until softened,

then spread smoothly. Sprinkle with hazelnuts, pressing them in lightly with your fingers.

Refrigerate until chocolate is firm. Invert candy onto a flat surface and break apart into small pieces (about 1½ inches square). Wrap airtight; store in a cool place (below 75°F) for up to 3 days. Makes about 3 dozen pieces.

HAZELNUT CHOCOLATE TRUFFLES

(Pictured on page 55)

Preparation time: About 2 hours, including chilling time
Storage time: Up to 10 days in refrigerator; up to 1 month in freezer

These candies have a creamy texture and a rich hazelnut flavor. For a spectacular presentation, give them in an edible chocolate box (page 54).

  1 **cup hazelnuts**
  ¾ **cup (¼ lb. plus ¼ cup) butter or margarine, melted**
  3 **ounces *each* semisweet chocolate and milk chocolate**
  5 **egg yolks**
  1 **cup unsifted powdered sugar**
  1 **teaspoon vanilla**
     Coatings: About 1 cup chocolate sprinkles, finely chopped nuts, or unsweetened cocoa or ground sweet chocolate (or use ⅓ cup of each)

Spread hazelnuts in a shallow baking pan and toast in a 350° oven until pale golden beneath skins (10 to 15 minutes), shaking pan occasionally. Pour nuts onto a towel and fold towel to enclose; rub briskly to remove as much of skins as possible. Discard skins; chop nuts.

Pour 6 tablespoons of the butter into a blender or food processor. Add chopped nuts and whirl until very smooth and creamy. Set aside.

In a small pan, heat remaining 6 tablespoons butter until bubbly and foamy. Remove from heat; add semisweet and milk chocolate. Stir until melted and smooth, then set aside.

In large bowl of an electric mixer, beat egg yolks until foamy. Gradually add sugar, beating until mixture is thick; add vanilla. With mixer on medium speed, add nut-butter mixture, 1 tablespoon at a time, beating well after each addition. Then begin mixing in warm chocolate mixture, 1 teaspoon at a time. After 6 teaspoons have been added, increase additions to 1 tablespoon; when all chocolate has been added, beat until mixture is smooth. Cover; refrigerate for 30 minutes.

Put your choice of coating in a small bowl. (Or use all 3 coatings, placing each in a separate bowl.) Scoop out rounded teaspoonfuls of the truffle mixture and form into balls, then roll in coating. Wrap airtight; store in refrigerator for up to 10 days, in freezer for up to 1 month. Makes 7 dozen truffles.

CHOCOLATE–FILLED EGGS

♥ ♥ ♥

Preparation time: 2 to 2½ hours, including chilling time
Storage time: Up to 2 weeks in refrigerator

You needn't be a pro to make these impressive Easter eggs—though they look so polished and professional, your friends will surely think they came from a fine candy shop! To make the eggs, you'll need inexpensive plastic egg molds, sold in sheets in cookware and candy supply stores.

> **Chocolate Pâté (page 54)**
> 8 **ounces white candy coating, coarsely chopped**
> **Chocolate for trim (directions follow)**

Prepare Chocolate Pâté and set aside at room temperature.

Place candy coating in the top of a double boiler over hot water. Stir just until half the coating is melted; then remove top of double boiler from water and stir until coating is completely melted. Let cool to lukewarm, stirring occasionally (20 to 30 minutes).

Wipe out molds with a clean, soft cloth. In 3-inch-long half-egg molds, place 1 tablespoon melted coating; use 1½ teaspoons for 2-inch-long molds. (If using molds cut crosswise, set them in an egg carton to hold upright.) With back of a small spoon, push coating up sides of molds to coat, as shown below left; add more coating if needed to

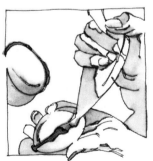

To form shells, push candy coating up sides of molds with back of a spoon (left); chill. To seal halves together, pipe chocolate around seam, using a pastry bag (right).

fill thin spots. Coating should be about ⅛ inch thick. Refrigerate until firm (10 to 15 minutes).

When shells are firm, spoon in pâté; use about 2½ tablespoons for 3-inch molds, about 1 tablespoon for 2-inch molds. Reserve remaining pâté. Freeze eggs level, in a single layer, until firm (20 to 30 minutes). When eggs are firm, invert on wax paper and tap back of mold lightly until eggs fall out. Spread 1 teaspoon reserved pâté over 1 egg half; at once press matching egg half on top. (Reserve remaining pâté for other uses.)

Place chocolate for trim in a pastry bag fitted with a small leaf tip. Pipe around seam where egg halves meet. Work fast; fingers will melt chocolate. Set eggs on a rack and refrigerate until trim is set (about 5 minutes). Cover airtight; store in refrigerator for up to 2 weeks. On gift tag, note that eggs are best if served at room temperature. Makes 4 or 5 (3-inch) eggs, 8 or 9 (2-inch) eggs.

CHOCOLATE FOR TRIM. Place 3 ounces **bittersweet or semisweet chocolate** (coarsely chopped) or ½ cup semisweet chocolate chips in the top of a double boiler over hot (but not simmering) water. Stir just until chocolate is melted. Let cool to 90°F.

APRICOT SLIMS

♥ ♥ ♥

Preparation time: 1 to 1¼ hours, including chilling time
Storage time: Up to 1 month in refrigerator

Tangy and refreshing, these candies combine dried apricots and coconut. Chopped almonds—blanched or unblanched—make a crunchy coating.

> 1 **package (6 oz.) moist-pack dried apricots**
> ⅓ **cup unsweetened grated or flaked coconut**
> 1 **tablespoon orange juice**
> **About ¼ cup finely chopped almonds**

Put apricots through a food chopper fitted with a fine blade. Add coconut and put through food chopper again. Stir in orange juice and mix well. (Or combine apricots, coconut, and orange juice in a food processor and whirl until mixture begins to hold together in a ball—about 1 minute.) Divide mixture into 4 equal parts and wrap each in wax paper or plastic wrap. Refrigerate until cold and easy to handle.

To shape each part, sprinkle about 1 tablespoon almonds on a board; roll apricot mixture back and forth with your palms over nuts, forming a 16-inch rope. Cut diagonally into 2-inch pieces. Wrap airtight and store in refrigerator for up to 1 month. Makes 32 pieces.

A hinged wooden box, lined with fabric and decorated
with a hand-cut stencil, is the perfect container for these Marzipan Fruit-Nut Candies
(facing page). For the prettiest presentation, roll marzipan
bonbons in chopped pistachios or other nuts; or use the almond-paste candy to fill your
favorite dried fruits.

MARZIPAN FRUIT-NUT CANDIES

(Pictured on facing page)

Preparation time: About 1¼ hours
Storage time: Up to 2 days at room temperature;
up to 1 month in refrigerator

Starting with marzipan, dried fruits, and crisp nuts, you can produce an assortment of appealing bonbons in no time. A selection like that shown on the facing page makes a really special gift box. For the best flavor, use only butter (not margarine) in the marzipan mixture.

> 1 can or package (8 oz.) almond paste
> ½ cup (¼ lb.) butter, at room temperature
> 3 cups unsifted powdered sugar
> Flavorings (optional): Vanilla, rum, brandy, cognac, kirsch, or coffee- or orange-flavored liqueur
> Fruits & nuts: Chopped nuts, pine nuts, walnut and/or pecan halves, moist-pack dried apricot halves, moist-pack pitted prunes, pitted dates, and dried figs (if necessary, split fruits to hold marzipan)

In a bowl, beat almond paste, butter, and sugar until smoothly blended. If desired, flavor marzipan by adding ¼ teaspoon vanilla or ½ teaspoon liquor or liqueur to each ½ cup marzipan mixture.

Take a bit of marzipan, roll it between your palms, and shape into a ball, log, or oval. Then roll in chopped nuts or pine nuts, or sandwich between nut halves. Or use marzipan to fill prunes or other fruit; decorate tops with nuts, if desired. (As you work, keep marzipan covered with plastic wrap.)

Wrap finished candies airtight and store at room temperature for up to 2 days, in refrigerator for up to 1 month. Makes 2⅓ cups marzipan (enough for 50 to 60 confections, each made with 2 teaspoons marzipan).

CARAMEL NUT CORN

Preparation time: About 40 minutes
Storage time: Up to 3 days at room temperature

This crunchy confection will have your friends clamoring for more—and our quick, simple method makes it easy to accommodate them!

> 4 quarts popped popcorn (about ¾ cup unpopped)
> 1 cup roasted, salted peanuts
> ½ cup (¼ lb.) butter or margarine
> ½ cup *each* molasses and firmly packed brown sugar

In a well-buttered 11- by 17-inch roasting pan, mix popcorn and peanuts. Set aside. Melt butter in a 1½- to 2-quart pan over medium-low heat; stir in molasses and sugar. Bring to a boil; boil gently, stirring often, for 5 minutes.

Immediately drizzle butter mixture over popcorn and peanuts; stir together. Bake, uncovered, in a 350° oven until browned (15 to 20 minutes), stirring every 5 minutes. Let cool completely. Package airtight and store at room temperature for up to 3 days. Makes about 4 quarts caramel corn.

PEANUT BUTTER–BROWN SUGAR FUDGE

Preparation time: About 30 minutes
Storage time: Up to 1 week in refrigerator

The world is full of peanut butter lovers—and any one of them would love to be surprised with a panful of this creamy fudge.

> 1 cup *each* granulated sugar and firmly packed brown sugar
> 2 tablespoons butter or margarine
> ½ cup evaporated milk
> ¼ cup creamy peanut butter
> 1 cup miniature marshmallows
> 1 teaspoon vanilla
> ¼ cup chopped dry-roasted peanuts

In a 3- to 4-quart pan, combine granulated sugar, brown sugar, butter, and evaporated milk. Bring to a boil over high heat, then boil until syrup reaches 234°F (soft ball stage) on a candy thermometer (about 5 minutes).

Add peanut butter and sprinkle in marshmallows; *do not stir.* Remove from heat and let cool to about 150°F. Add vanilla. With a wooden spoon, beat vigorously until mixture is creamy and loses its shiny appearance (about 5 minutes).

Quickly spread in a well-buttered 8- or 9-inch square pan. Sprinkle peanuts over top and press in lightly. Let stand, uncovered, until firm; cut into 1-inch squares. Wrap airtight and store in refrigerator for up to 1 week. Makes 5 to 7 dozen pieces.

SWEET & SAVORY PRESERVES

Tasty & colorful jams, jellies, pickles & relishes

An elegant decanter of apricot cordial, a jar of sparkling pomegranate jelly, a container of marinated tiny carrots from your garden—these are just a few of the tempting gift ideas in this chapter. You'll find plenty of surprises here—especially if you think that home canning requires hours in the kitchen and produces only the familiar cucumber pickles and fruit preserves. Recipes like our Refrigerator Corn Relish and No-cook Freezer Jam go together in a jiffy. And in addition to tried-and-true favorites, you'll find jams and jellies made from figs, kiwis, mangoes, and even garlic and jalapeño chiles; for pickling, you can choose anything from oranges to melon to zucchini. We also offer a wealth of specialty items: sweet Dried Fruit Cordials, intense Italian Fruit Syrups, spicy mustards, and flavored vinegars.

Home-canned goodies are as appealing to look at as they are delicious. Decorative glass containers show off the foods' bright colors beautifully; if you like, you can top a jar with pretty fabric or a doily and ribbon, as shown on page 31, and add a handmade label and tag.

Ruby Wine Jelly

♥ ♥ ♥

Preparation time: About 15 minutes
Storage time: Up to 2 years in a cool place

For the wine lovers among your friends, make a batch of this full-flavored, burgundy-colored jelly to serve with beef or lamb.

- 1¾ **cups ruby port**
- ¾ **cup claret or other dry red wine, such as Cabernet Sauvignon**
- 3 **cups sugar**
- 1 **pouch (3 oz.) liquid pectin**

Prepare five ½-pint canning jars as directed for Short-cook Jam (page 62).

In a 3- to 4-quart pan, combine port, claret, and sugar. Stir over low heat until sugar is completely dissolved (about 5 minutes). Stir in pectin all at once; if foam forms on top, skim it off. Fill prepared, hot jars with jelly to within ⅛ inch of rims. Wipe rims clean; top with hot lids, then firmly screw on rings.

Process jars of jelly as directed for Short-cook Jam (page 62). Let cool on a towel, away from drafts. Test for seals as directed on page 62. Store in a cool place for up to 2 years. Makes 5 cups.

Honey Jelly

♥ ♥ ♥

Preparation time: 10 to 15 minutes
Storage time: Up to 2 years in a cool place

This mellow combination of honey and apple juice makes a sparkling topping for toast or muffins.

- 1¾ **cups honey**
- 1 **cup apple juice**
- 1 **tablespoon lemon juice**
- 1 **pouch (3 oz.) liquid pectin**

Prepare three ½-pint canning jars as directed for Short-cook Jam (page 62).

In a 3- to 4-quart pan, combine honey, apple juice, and lemon juice. Bring to a boil over high heat; immediately stir in pectin. Bring to a rolling boil that cannot be stirred down, then boil for 1 minute, stirring constantly. Remove from heat and skim off foam.

Fill prepared, hot jars with jelly to within ⅛ inch of rims. Wipe rims clean; top with hot lids, then firmly screw on rings.

Process jars of jelly as directed for Short-cook Jam (page 62). Let cool on a towel, away from drafts. Test for seals as directed on page 62. Store in a cool place for up to 2 years. Makes 3 cups.

Pomegranate Jelly

♥ ♥ ♥

Preparation time: About 2 hours, including time to drain juice from pomegranate purée
Storage time: Up to 2 years in a cool place

Pomegranate seeds provide the juice for this sweet-tart red jelly. Submerging the fruit in water makes it quite easy to separate seeds from peel and pulp, but it's still wise to allow extra time for preparation—you'll need almost a quart of juice.

- **About 10 large pomegranates**
- 2 **tablespoons lemon juice**
- 1 **pouch (3 oz.) liquid pectin**
- 6 **cups sugar**

Cut crown end off each pomegranate and lightly score peel lengthwise down sides, dividing fruit into quarters. Immerse fruit in a bowl of cool water and let soak for 5 minutes. Holding fruit under water, break sections apart with your fingers and separate seeds from pulp; as you work, seeds will sink and pulp and peel will float. Skim off pulp and peel; discard. Scoop up seeds and drain in a colander; let dry on paper towels.

Whirl 1½ to 2 cups pomegranate seeds at a time in a blender until liquefied. Set a colander in a bowl; line colander with moistened cheesecloth. Pour in pomegranate purée and let juice drip through cloth. To speed the process, gather edges of cloth with rubber-gloved hands and twist *slowly* (juice tends to squirt) to extract liquid. You need 3½ cups juice *total*.

Prepare seven ½-pint canning jars as directed for Short-cook Jam (page 62).

In a 5- to 6-quart pan, combine pomegranate juice, lemon juice, and sugar. Over medium-high heat, bring to a rolling boil. Add pectin and stir to blend; bring to a rolling boil that cannot be stirred down, then boil for 1 minute. Remove from heat and skim off foam.

Fill prepared, hot jars with jelly to within ⅛ inch of rims. Wipe rims clean; top with hot lids, then firmly screw on rings.

Process jars of jelly as directed for Short-cook Jam (page 62). Let cool on a towel, away from drafts. Test for seals as directed on page 62. Store in a cool place for up to 2 years. Makes about 7 cups.

Quick-and-Easy Fruit Jams

For year-round giving, nothing is better than homemade fruit jam. And with our no-fuss methods, you can easily make plenty. The short-cook technique uses dry pectin and a 2-minute cooking time; it's well suited to low-acid fruits such as figs, mangoes, papayas, peaches, and pears. Fresh-tasting freezer jam, made with liquid pectin, requires no cooking—but it needs more sugar to jell, so for best results, choose tart fruits such as apricots, berries, kiwi fruit, nectarines, and plums.

Whichever procedure you use, keep two rules in mind: *you can't double jam recipes, and you can't reduce the amount of sugar.* If you do either, you may end up with fruit syrup instead of jam!

SHORT-COOK JAM

Fruit of your choice
(see chart)

Lemon juice (see chart)

1 box (1¾ or 2 oz.) dry
pectin

Sugar (see chart)

To prepare jars: Check yield for each fruit to determine how many canning jars you will need. Check jars carefully; discard any with nicked or cracked rims. Wash jars in hot, soapy water; rinse well. Immerse jars, rings, and new lids in boiling water to cover; hold at a gentle boil for 10 to 30 minutes. When you are ready to fill jars, drain them on a clean towel.

Meanwhile, rinse fruit; then peel, seed, hull, or core as necessary. Cut fruit into cubes. Mash fruit with a potato masher (or whirl briefly in a food processor, but do not purée).

In an 8- to 10-quart pan, mix fruit, lemon juice, and pectin. Place over high heat; stirring constantly, bring to a rolling boil that cannot be stirred down. Still stirring, add sugar. Return to a boil that cannot be stirred down, then boil for exactly 2 minutes. Remove from heat; skim off foam.

Ladle hot jam into prepared, hot jars; fill to within ¼ inch of rims for 1-pint jars, to within ⅛ inch of rims for ½-pint jars. Wipe rims clean. Lift lids from hot water and immediately place on jars; firmly screw on rings.

To process: Place jars on a rack in a canning or other deep kettle. Add boiling water to cover jars. Hold at simmering (180°F) for 10 minutes. Remove from water; let cool on a towel, away from drafts.

To test for a seal: Press center of lid. If it stays down, seal is good; if it pops when pressed, there's no seal. Refrigerate unsealed jars and use as soon as possible. Store sealed jars in a dark, cool (50°F) place for up to 2 years.

NO-COOK FREEZER JAM

Fruit of your choice
(see chart)

Sugar (see chart)

1 pouch (3 oz.) liquid
pectin

Lemon juice (see chart)

Rinse fruit; then peel, seed, hull, or core as necessary. Cut fruit into cubes. Mash fruit with a potato masher (or whirl briefly in a food processor, but do not purée).

In a large bowl, thoroughly mix fruit and sugar; let stand for 10 minutes, stirring occasionally. Meanwhile, mix pectin and lemon juice; add to fruit mixture and stir (don't beat in air) for 3 minutes. Fill clean small canning jars or freezer containers with jam, leaving ½ inch headspace. Add lids. Let jam stand at room temperature until next day; then store in refrigerator for up to 3 weeks, in freezer for up to 1 year.

SHORT-COOK METHOD (1¼- or 2-oz. box)

FRUIT	AMT. OF FRUIT	MASHED FRUIT	LEMON JUICE	SUGAR	YIELD
Fig	3¼ lbs.	5 c. + ½ c. water	½ c.	7 c.	8½ c.
Mango	6 lbs.	4 c.	¼ c.	6 c.	6½ c.
Papaya	5 lbs.	4 c.	¼ c.	6 c.	6½ c.
Peach	3 lbs.	4 c.	¼ c.	6 c.	6¾ c.
Pear	3 lbs.	4 c.	¼ c.	5½ c.	6½ c.

NO-COOK FREEZER METHOD (3-oz. pouch)

FRUIT	AMT. OF FRUIT	MASHED FRUIT	LEMON JUICE	SUGAR	YIELD
Apricot	1 lb.	1½ c.	¼ c.	3 c.	4 c.
Berry	1 qt.	2 c.	2 T.	4 c.	4¾ c.
Kiwi	1¼ lbs.	2¼ c.	¼ c.	4 c.	5 c.
Nectarine	1 lb.	1½ c.	¼ c.	3 c.	4 c.
Plum	1¼ lbs.	2¼ c.	2 T.	4 c.	5 c

Our fruit jams (facing page) go beyond the ordinary
peach and berry to include such exotic flavors as fig, mango, papaya, kiwi, and pear. If
you like, dress up each jar with a fabric square and a
raffia or cornhusk "ribbon."

GARLIC OR SHALLOT JELLY

♥ ♥ ♥

Preparation time: 24 to 36 hours to flavor vinegar;
about 20 minutes to make jelly
Storage time: Up to 2 years in a cool place

When you open a jar of this crystal-clear jelly, you're in for a surprise: the bold aroma and flavor of garlic or shallots. Tart yet sweet, the jelly is a wonderful relish for beef, lamb, or chicken; it's also good with cream cheese and crackers.

½ **cup finely chopped garlic or shallots**
  About 3 cups white wine vinegar
2 **cups water**
6 **cups sugar**
2 **pouches (3 oz. *each*) liquid pectin**

Combine garlic or shallots and 3 cups of the vinegar in a 2- to 2½-quart pan over medium heat. Simmer gently, uncovered, for 15 minutes. Remove from heat and pour into a glass jar. Cover and let stand at room temperature for 24 to 36 hours; then pour through a fine strainer into a bowl, pressing garlic or shallots with the back of a spoon to squeeze out as much liquid as possible. Discard residue. Measure liquid; if necessary, add or reduce vinegar to make 2 cups.

Prepare seven ½-pint canning jars as directed for Short-cook Jam (page 62).

In a 5- to 6-quart pan, combine flavored vinegar, water, and sugar. Bring to a rolling boil over medium-high heat. Stir in pectin and bring to a rolling boil that cannot be stirred down. Boil, stirring constantly, for 1 minute. Remove from heat and skim off foam.

Fill prepared, hot jars with jelly to within ⅛ inch of rims. Wipe rims clean; top with hot lids, then firmly screw on rings.

Process jars of jelly as directed for Short-cook Jam (page 62). Let cool on a towel, away from drafts. Test for seals as directed on page 62. Store in a cool place for up to 2 years. Makes 7 cups.

RED PEPPER JELLY

♥ ♥ ♥

Preparation time: About 30 minutes
Storage time: Up to 2 years in a cool place

Like Garlic or Shallot Jelly (above), this mild-flavored red jelly tastes great with meat and atop crackers spread with cream cheese.

4 **large red bell peppers, seeded and cut into pieces**
2½ **cups white wine vinegar**
6 **cups sugar**
2 **pouches (3 oz. *each*) liquid pectin**

Prepare six ½-pint canning jars as directed for Short-cook Jam (page 62).

Place cut-up bell peppers in a blender or food processor and whirl until finely chopped. Pour into a 5- to 6-quart pan and stir in vinegar and sugar until well blended. Bring to a rolling boil over high heat, stirring constantly. Pour in pectin all at once, bring to a rolling boil that cannot be stirred down, and boil for 1 minute, stirring constantly. Remove from heat and skim off foam.

Fill prepared, hot jars with jelly to within ⅛ inch of rims. Wipe rims clean; top with hot lids, then firmly screw on rings.

Process jars of jelly as directed for Short-cook Jam (page 62). Let cool on a towel, away from drafts. Test for seals as directed on page 62. Store in a cool place for up to 2 years. Makes 6 cups.

JALAPEÑO JELLY

♥ ♥ ♥

Preparation time: 25 to 30 minutes
Storage time: Up to 2 years in a cool place

For something a little different, give hot, spicy jalapeño jelly—a delightful Southwest-style condiment for chicken, pork, ham, or beef.

¼ **cup chopped jalapeño chiles (4 to 6 medium-size chiles; remove half the seeds before chopping)**
¾ **cup chopped green bell pepper**
6 **cups sugar**
2½ **cups cider vinegar**
2 **pouches (3 oz. *each*) liquid pectin**

Prepare seven ½-pint canning jars as directed for Short-cook Jam (page 62).

In a blender or food processor, whirl chiles and bell pepper until finely ground (or put through a food chopper fitted with a fine blade). Put ground vegetables and any juice in a 5- to 6-quart pan; stir in sugar and vinegar.

Bring to a rolling boil over high heat, stirring constantly. Pour in pectin all at once, bring to a rolling boil that cannot be stirred down, and boil for 1 minute, stirring constantly. Remove from heat and skim off foam. Fill prepared, hot jars with jelly to within ⅛ inch of rims. Wipe rims clean; top with hot lids, then firmly screw on rings.

Process jars of jelly as directed for Short-cook Jam (page 62). Let cool on a towel, away from drafts. Test for seals as directed on page 62. Store in a cool place for up to 2 years. Makes 7 cups.

SPICY TOMATO JELLY

♥ ♥ ♥

Preparation time: 1½ to 1¾ hours, including time to strain tomato juice
Storage time: Up to 2 years in a cool place

Rosy pink and spicy-sweet, this unusual jelly makes an especially nice accompaniment for pork, lamb, and poultry.

    About 3¼ pounds (about 7 large) ripe tomatoes, cut into quarters
1   cup water
1   whole nutmeg, lightly crushed
2   cinnamon sticks (*each* about 3 inches long), broken into pieces
1½ teaspoons whole cloves
½   teaspoon ground allspice
¾   teaspoon red food color (optional)
¼   cup cider vinegar
1   box (1¾ or 2 oz.) dry pectin
4½ cups sugar

In a 4- to 5-quart pan, combine tomatoes, water, nutmeg, cinnamon sticks, cloves, allspice, food color (if used), and vinegar. Bring to a boil; reduce heat, cover, and simmer, stirring occasionally, until tomatoes break apart into a sauce (about 45 minutes).

Press tomato mixture through a wire strainer; discard residue. Return juice to pan; bring to a boil. Set a wire strainer in a bowl; line strainer with moistened cheesecloth. Pour in hot tomato juice and let drain, stirring occasionally, until residue left on cheesecloth is dry (about 30 minutes). Meanwhile, prepare six ½-pint canning jars as directed for Short-cook Jam (page 62).

Measure tomato juice; you should have 3 cups. If necessary, add water or boil juice down to make this amount. Combine juice and pectin in a 4- to 5-quart pan; bring to a boil, stirring occasionally. Add sugar all at once; bring to a rolling boil that cannot be stirred down. Boil for 1 minute, stirring constantly. (If using a 2-oz. box of pectin, boil for 2 minutes.) Remove from heat; let stand for 1 minute. Carefully skim off foam. Fill prepared, hot jars with jelly to within ⅛ inch of rims. Wipe rims clean; top with hot lids, then firmly screw on rings.

Process jars of jelly as directed for Short-cook Jam (page 62). Let cool on a towel, away from drafts. Test for seals as directed on page 62. Store in a cool place for up to 2 years. Makes 6 cups.

BITTERSWEET MARMALADE

♥ ♥ ♥

Preparation time: About 1½ hours
Storage time: Up to 2 years in a cool place

This pretty amber-colored marmalade combines the sweet-tart juices and peels of three citrus fruits: oranges, lemons, and grapefruit. (We also offer a version made with kumquats.)

6   medium-size thin-skinned oranges (such as Valencia)
2   thin-skinned lemons
2   medium-size thin-skinned grapefruit
2   cups water
9   cups sugar

Wash oranges, lemons, and grapefruit, but do not peel. Cut crosswise into ⅛-inch-thick slices; discard seeds and end pieces. Cut orange and lemon slices into quarters; cut grapefruit slices into eighths.

Place fruit and water in a 6- to 8-quart pan. Bring mixture to a boil; reduce heat, cover, and simmer until peel is translucent and tender when pierced (25 to 30 minutes). Add sugar and stir until well blended. Cook over medium-high heat, uncovered, stirring often, for 30 minutes or until mixture thickens and reaches jell point (228°F on a candy thermometer, or until 1 tablespoon of juice jells when refrigerated for 3 minutes).

Meanwhile, prepare eight 1-pint canning jars as directed for Short-cook Jam (page 62).

Fill prepared, hot jars with marmalade to within ¼ inch of rims. Wipe rims clean; top with hot lids, then firmly screw on rings.

Process jars of marmalade as directed for Short-cook Jam (page 62). Let cool on a towel, away from drafts. Test for seals as directed on page 62. Store in a cool place for up to 2 years. Makes 8 pints.

♥ KUMQUAT MARMALADE

Follow directions for **Bittersweet Marmalade,** but substitute 9 cups thinly sliced **kumquats** for oranges, lemons, and grapefruit. Add water; cook until fruit is tender when pierced (20 minutes). Add sugar and complete marmalade as directed.

Fresh summer fruits are juiced or puréed, then
fermented with yeast to make intensely flavored Italian Fruit Syrups (facing page)
in jewel-like colors. Shown here are blueberry,
orange, raspberry, lemon, and lime syrups.

ITALIAN FRUIT SYRUPS

(Pictured on facing page)

♥ ♥ ♥

Preparation time: 2 to 4 days to ferment syrups;
1 to 1½ hours to prepare and bottle
Storage time: Up to 1 year in refrigerator

Capture the essence of ripe summer fruit with these enticing syrups. In Italy, they're mixed with sparkling water or white wine for a refreshing drink, or frozen to make sorbet-like *granitas.* The syrups are delicious over ice cream, too.

Because these syrups are fermented, their flavor is especially intense. The yeast-fruit mixture, which bubbles and froths for several days, looks dull at first; but when you cook it before bottling, it brightens and takes on a jewel-like clarity. To show off the color, give the syrups in tall glass bottles. Be sure to include suggestions for use on the gift tag.

2 pounds ripe strawberries, raspberries, blueberries, peaches, or plums, rinsed and drained; or 2 cups orange, lemon, or lime juice

2 packages active dry yeast

1 teaspoon sugar (if using lemon or lime juice)

Sugar, water, and lemon juice (amounts for each fruit or juice choice follow)

Choose fruit or juice from the list above. Hull strawberries; pit (but do not peel) and slice peaches or plums. Then purée fruit in a food processor or blender. Press raspberry purée through a fine strainer to remove seeds. Measure purée; you need the amounts listed at right for each fruit.

Pour purée or juice into a 3-quart or larger glass, ceramic, or stainless steel bowl. Sprinkle with yeast; if using lemon or lime juice, add 1 teaspoon sugar. Stir to moisten yeast. Cover bowl with a cloth or paper towel and set aside at room temperature to ferment, stirring occasionally. Mixture will bubble and rise in bowl. When bubbles no longer appear when mixture is stirred, fermentation is complete (allow about 2 days for juices, 3 to 4 days for purées).

Line a colander with 3 or 4 thicknesses of moistened cheesecloth, making sure cloths are large enough to hang over sides of colander. Set colander over a 6- to 8-quart stainless steel, porcelain, or enamel-coated metal pan. Pour purée or juice through cheesecloth; draw together corners of cheesecloth and twist cloth to extract juice. (You may have to scrape purée from cloth in order to force out as much juice as possible.) Discard pulp and any seeds; remove colander from pan.

To pan, add sugar, water, and lemon juice as specified for each fruit or juice. Bring to a boil over high heat; boil, uncovered, until reduced to amount specified for each fruit or juice (15 to 20 minutes).

Let syrup cool completely, then pour into a 1- to 2-quart glass container. Cover tightly and store in refrigerator for up to 1 year. A harmless sediment may form at bottom of container; to preserve clarity, do not shake. Makes 3½ to 7 cups, depending on fruit or juice used.

Strawberries (you should have 2½ to 2¾ cups purée). Use 6 cups **sugar,** 4 cups **water,** and 1½ cups **lemon juice;** boil down to 7 cups.

Blueberries, plums, or peaches (you should have about 2 cups purée). Use 4½ cups **sugar,** 3 cups **water,** and 1 cup plus 2 tablespoons **lemon juice;** boil down to 5¼ cups.

Orange, lemon, or lime juice (2 cups). Use 4½ cups **sugar** and 3 cups **water.** *For orange juice only,* also add 1 cup plus 2 tablespoons **lemon juice.** Boil down to 5¼ cups.

Raspberries (you should have 1½ cups strained purée). Use 3 cups **sugar,** 2 cups **water,** and ¾ cup **lemon juice;** boil down to 3½ cups.

♥ WATER COOLER

Partially fill an 8- to 10-ounce glass with **ice.** Add **sparkling or plain water** and 2 to 4 tablespoons (or to taste) **Italian Fruit Syrup.** Makes 1 serving.

♥ ITALIAN WINE COOLER

Add 1 to 2 tablespoons (or to taste) **Italian Fruit Syrup** to 4 to 5 ounces chilled **dry white wine.** Makes 1 serving.

♥ GRANITA

Combine equal parts **water** and **Italian Fruit Syrup.** Freeze until almost hard. With an electric mixer or a food processor, beat to a coarse slush; serve between courses or as a dessert.

♥ FRUIT SYRUP SUNDAE

Pour 1 to 2 tablespoons **Italian Fruit Syrup** over a scoop of **vanilla ice cream,** fruit sherbet, or fruit ice. Makes 1 serving.

Garden Lemon Syrup

♥ ♥ ♥

Preparation time: About 15 minutes
Storage time: Up to 10 days in refrigerator; up to 3 months in freezer

This sweet, lemony syrup is especially flavorful when made with mild-tasting lemons from your garden. It's good on pancakes, waffles, or ice cream; you can also stir it into chilled sparkling water for a refreshing beverage. Note that if you want a completely clear syrup, you'll need to start by straining the lemon juice through 3 or 4 thicknesses of cheesecloth.

   2 cups lemon juice
   3 cups sugar
   ½ teaspoon butter or margarine

In a heavy 5-quart pan, combine lemon juice, sugar, and butter. Bring to a boil over medium heat, stirring until sugar is dissolved. Then reduce heat and simmer, uncovered, for 6 minutes, stirring often. Remove from heat and let cool. Pour into canning jars or freezer containers, leaving ½ inch headspace. Cover tightly; store in refrigerator for up to 10 days, in freezer for up to 3 months. Makes about 3½ cups.

Quick Lemon or Lime Curd

♥ ♥ ♥

Preparation time: 25 to 30 minutes
Storage time: Up to 1 year in a cool place

A traditional English spread for scones, this tart-sweet preserve has a texture and flavor much like that of lemon pie filling. (For a nontraditional variation, use lime peel and juice in place of lemon.)

   4 teaspoons grated lemon or lime peel
   ⅔ cup lemon or lime juice
   5 eggs
   1 cup sugar
   ½ cup (¼ lb.) butter or margarine, melted

Prepare three ½-pint canning jars as directed for Short-cook Jam (page 62).

   Combine lemon peel, lemon juice, eggs, and sugar in a blender; whirl until well blended. With blender on lowest speed, gradually add butter in a thin stream. Transfer mixture to a small, heavy pan. Cook over low heat, stirring constantly, until

mixture is thick enough to mound slightly when dropped from a spoon (6 to 8 minutes).

   Fill prepared, hot jars with lemon curd to within ⅛ inch of rims. Wipe rims clean; top with hot lids, then firmly screw on rings. Process jars of lemon curd as directed for Short-cook Jam (page 62). Let cool on a towel, away from drafts. Test for seals as directed on page 62. Store in a cool place for up to 1 year. Makes 3 cups.

Apricot Butter

♥ ♥ ♥

Preparation time: 45 to 60 minutes
Storage time: Up to 2 years in a cool place

Apricots give this variation on classic apple butter an appealingly different character.

   3 pounds apricots, pitted
   ¼ cup lemon juice
   3 cups sugar

Prepare five ½-pint canning jars as directed for Short-cook Jam (page 62).

   Whirl apricots, a few at a time, in a blender or food processor until smoothly puréed; you should have about 4 cups. Pour purée into a 4-quart pan; stir in lemon juice and sugar until well blended. Bring mixture to a boil over high heat, stirring constantly. Continue to boil, uncovered, stirring frequently, until thickened (15 to 18 minutes).

   Fill prepared, hot jars with apricot butter to within ⅛ inch of rims. Wipe rims clean; top with hot lids, then firmly screw on rings.

   Process jars of apricot butter as directed for Short-cook Jam (page 62). Let cool on a towel, away from drafts. Test for seals as directed on page 62. Store in a cool place for up to 2 years. Makes 5 cups.

Apple Butter

♥ ♥ ♥

Preparation time: 2½ to 3 hours
Storage time: Up to 2 years in a cool place

Slow, even cooking brings out the full flavor of this chunky, old-fashioned butter. If sweet Golden Delicious apples aren't available, you can use a tarter variety such as McIntosh, Jonathan, or Granny Smith, but you may want to add about ¼ cup more sugar.

4 cups apple juice or cider
12 medium-size Golden Delicious apples
(about 4 lbs. *total*), peeled, cored, and
sliced
1½ cups sugar
2 teaspoons ground cinnamon

In a heavy 4- to 5-quart pan, bring apple juice to a boil over high heat. Add apples; reduce heat and simmer, uncovered, stirring occasionally, until apples are soft enough to mash easily (about 45 minutes).

Stir in sugar and cinnamon until well blended. Cook over medium-low heat, uncovered, mashing apples and stirring frequently, until mixture is thick and reduced to 5 cups (1½ to 2 hours).

Meanwhile, prepare five ½-pint canning jars as directed for Short-cook Jam (page 62).

Fill prepared, hot jars with apple butter to within ⅛ inch of rims. Wipe rims clean; top with hot lids, then firmly screw on rings.

Process jars of apple butter as directed for Short-cook Jam (page 62). Let cool on a towel, away from drafts. Test for seals as directed on page 62. Store in a cool place for up to 2 years. Makes 5 cups.

RHUBARB CONSERVE

♥ ♥ ♥

Preparation time: 1 hour, plus 8 to 12 hours to stand
Storage time: Up to 2 years in a cool place

Rhubarb and citrus give this chunky conserve its tangy flavor; dates and raisins add sweetness. Serve with meats, over ice cream, or on toast.

2½ pounds rhubarb
5½ cups sugar
2 oranges
1 lemon
1½ cups *each* raisins and snipped
pitted dates
1 cup chopped walnuts

Wash rhubarb; cut off leaf and root ends, then dice stalks to make 4 cups. Place rhubarb in a 5-quart pan; stir in sugar until well blended. Cover and let stand at room temperature for 8 to 12 hours.

Wash unpeeled oranges and lemon; thinly slice. Remove seeds, then cut slices into small pieces. Add oranges, lemon, raisins, and dates to rhubarb mixture. Bring to a boil; reduce heat and simmer, uncovered, stirring occasionally, until thickened (35 to 40 minutes). About 5 minutes before removing from heat, stir in walnuts.

Meanwhile, prepare ten ½-pint canning jars as directed for Short-cook Jam (page 62).

Fill prepared, hot jars with conserve to within ⅛ inch of rims. Wipe rims clean; top with hot lids, then firmly screw on rings.

Process jars of conserve as directed for Short-cook Jam (page 62). Let cool on a towel, away from drafts. Test for seals as directed on page 62. Store in a cool place for up to 2 years. Makes 10 cups.

MANGO-APRICOT-DATE CHUTNEY

♥ ♥ ♥

Preparation time: About 1½ hours
Storage time: Up to 2 years in a cool place

Because this chutney features dried fruits, it's a good gift to make at any time of year. (Asian markets sell the dried mangoes you'll need, as well as preserved and pickled ginger.)

3½ cups water
½ pound *each* dried mangoes and dried
apricots; or 1 pound dried apricots
¾ cup *each* golden raisins and currants
1¼ cups pitted dates, coarsely snipped or
chopped
1½ cups white wine vinegar
1¼ cups firmly packed brown sugar
1 cup preserved ginger in syrup or pickled
ginger, drained and coarsely chopped
1 tablespoon mustard seeds
1½ teaspoons chili powder
Salt

In a 5- to 6-quart pan, combine water and mangoes. Bring to a simmer; cover and cook for 5 minutes. Add apricots and continue to simmer, covered, for 5 more minutes. (If using all apricots, simmer for only 5 minutes *total*.) Add raisins, currants, dates, vinegar, sugar, ginger, mustard seeds, and chili powder. Simmer, uncovered, stirring more frequently as mixture thickens, until almost all liquid has evaporated and chutney is thick (45 to 60 minutes). Season to taste with salt.

While chutney is cooking, prepare seven ½-pint canning jars as directed for Short-cook Jam (page 62). Fill prepared, hot jars with chutney to within ⅛ inch of rims. Wipe rims clean; top with hot lids, then firmly screw on rings.

Process jars of chutney as directed for Short-cook Jam (page 62). Let cool on a towel, away from drafts. Test for seals as directed on page 62. Store in a cool place for up to 2 years. Makes 7 cups.

CRANBERRY-RAISIN CHUTNEY

♥ ♥ ♥

Preparation time: 1 to 1¼ hours
Storage time: Up to 2 weeks in refrigerator; up to 6 months in freezer

Raisins, apple, honey, and spices balance the tartness of cranberries in this ruby-red sauce. A packet of whole spices flavors the simmering chutney; the longer you leave it in, the stronger the spice flavor will be.

- ½ teaspoon whole allspice
- 10 whole cloves
- 1 cinnamon stick (about 3 inches long)
- 4 cups fresh or frozen cranberries
- ¾ cup raisins
- ½ cup *each* thawed frozen apple juice concentrate and honey
- 6 tablespoons cider vinegar
- ¼ cup water
- 1 tablespoon minced fresh ginger
- ¼ teaspoon ground red pepper (cayenne)
- ½ cup *each* finely chopped onion and thinly sliced celery
- 1 small tart apple, peeled, cored, and chopped

Tie allspice, cloves, and cinnamon stick in a washed square of cheesecloth; set aside.

In a 3- to 4-quart pan, combine cranberries, raisins, apple juice concentrate, honey, vinegar, and water; cook over medium heat, uncovered, until berries begin to pop (about 10 minutes).

Add spice packet, ginger, red pepper, onion, celery, and apple. Simmer, uncovered, until apple is very soft and almost all liquid has evaporated (about 40 minutes). Discard spice packet; let chutney cool. (Or discard spices after cooling.) Ladle chutney into about four ½-pint canning jars or freezer containers, leaving 1 inch headspace. Cover tightly; store in refrigerator for up to 2 weeks, in freezer for up to 6 months. Makes about 4 cups.

MULLED CRANBERRIES

♥ ♥ ♥

Preparation time: 20 to 25 minutes
Storage time: Up to 1 week in refrigerator

Here's a quick-to-make hostess gift that's just right for Thanksgiving or Christmas—a pretty jar of bright cranberries flavored with cinnamon and orange liqueur. They're a festive accompaniment for any holiday roast, from turkey to pork.

In a 3- to 4-quart pan, combine 3 cups **fresh or frozen cranberries**, 1⅓ cups **sugar**, 6 tablespoons **orange-flavored liqueur**, and 2 **cinnamon sticks** (*each* about 3 inches long). Cover and cook over low heat, stirring gently to dissolve sugar, until berries are translucent (about 15 minutes). Let cool slightly; cover and store in refrigerator for up to 1 week. Pack into glass jars for giving (remove cinnamon sticks, if desired). Makes about 3 cups.

DRIED FRUIT CORDIALS

(Pictured on facing page)

♥ ♥ ♥

Preparation time: About 15 minutes, plus at least 1 week for cordials to mellow
Storage time: Up to 6 weeks at room temperature for fruit-cordial mixture; cordial alone keeps indefinitely

Dried apricots, peaches, pears, or prunes soaked in a mixture of sweetened white wine and brandy make fruity cordials that mellow with age. Because the fruit softens any harshness, you can use inexpensive wine and brandy—but do be sure to present the cordials in handsome decanters to show off their colors. On the gift tag, note that the liqueur is for sipping, the soaked fruit for enjoying on ice cream or pound cake.

- 1 pound dried apricots, prunes with pits, pears, or peaches
- 1 bottle (750 ml.) or 3⅓ cups dry white wine
- 1 cup brandy
- 2 cups sugar

Place fruit in a glass, ceramic, or stainless steel container. Stir in wine, brandy, and sugar until well blended. Cover tightly. Let stand at room temperature for at least 1 week to allow flavors to develop; stir occasionally for the first few days to dissolve sugar.

After 1 week, apricots, prunes, and pears should be soft; peaches should still be slightly firm. After 3 to 4 weeks, the cordial's fruit flavor will reach maximum intensity.

To give, repack fruit and cordial together in 1 large or 2 small decanters or other glass containers. On the gift tag, note that after about 6 weeks, fruit should be removed if it has become too soft. Cordial alone will keep indefinitely. Makes about 6 cups fruit-cordial mixture.

Simple-to-make Dried Fruit Cordials (facing page)
look their elegant best in glass decanters. On the gift tag, suggest serving the liqueur for
after-dinner sipping; the saturated fruit—pears,
peaches, apricots, or prunes—is delicious on ice cream or cake.

FRESH FRUIT LEATHER

♥ ♥ ♥

Preparation time: About 30 minutes, plus 5 to 10 hours to dry
Storage time: Up to 2 months in a cool, dry place; up to 1 year in freezer

Sheets of dried fresh fruit purée are delicious snacks—and very appropriate gifts for the cross-country skier or backpacker on your list. Leathers are especially easy to make in an electric dehydrator, but you can also sun-dry them successfully if the temperature is 85°F or higher, with relative humidity below 60 percent.

To gift-wrap fruit leathers, just bundle several plastic-wrapped rolls together and tie with a ribbon.

Fruit Purée (choices and directions follow)

Prepare drying surface for dehydrator- or sun-drying.

For dehydrator-drying, cover each drying tray with a sheet of plastic wrap, extending it over edges; secure wrap with tape. Or prepare special trays for leather (sold with some dehydrators) as directed by manufacturer. Preheat dehydrator.

For sun-drying, start early in the day. Cover shallow pans, such as rimmed 10- by 15-inch baking pans, with plastic wrap; extend wrap over edges and secure with tape. Set pans on a level surface, such as a table, in full sun.

Prepare fruit purée (or purées) of your choice. Pour each 1 cup of purée onto prepared surface and spread to about 10 inches square (layer of purée should be ⅛ to ¼ inch thick). To dry evenly without brittle edges, purée should be slightly thicker around edges than in center.

Dry purée until leathery, pliable, and no longer tacky to touch; it should peel off drying surface with no sticky spots. Most purées dry in 5 to 10 hours. *If sun-drying purée,* keep purée clean by suspending cheesecloth over top, supported by 2-by-4s placed on each side. If purée isn't dry by day's end, bring indoors; return to sun the next day.

While fruit leather is still slightly warm, you can cut it into snack-size strips. Wrap each piece in plastic wrap. Store flat or roll up, enclosing the wrap. Place inside a paper bag; seal bag with tape (paper absorbs any moisture). Store in a cool, dry, dark place for up to 2 months, in freezer for up to 1 year. Each cup of purée makes a 10-inch square of fruit leather.

FRUIT PURÉE. Peeling most fruits is optional, but peeled fruits make smoother leather. To prepare fruit for puréeing, wash unpeeled fruit, using a mild soap or detergent; rinse well and dry.

Rinse berries in cool water; drain on paper towels. To purée, whirl fruit (plus lemon juice, spices, or sweetener, as noted below) in a blender until very smooth, pushing it into blades as needed; if fruit is quite juicy, you can purée it in a food processor.

Because drying concentrates natural sugars, many fruits don't need added sweetening. If you plan to store leathers at room temperature, sweeten them with honey or corn syrup; sugar-sweetened leathers may become grainy-textured. For freezer storage or to eat within a few weeks, use sugar if you prefer.

Each fruit choice below yields 1 cup purée.

Apple. Gravensteins, which are juicy, need not be cooked. For other market varieties, follow cooking directions for pulpy apples.

Juicy apples. Core and slice **apples** to make about 2 cups. Purée with 1 tablespoon **lemon juice,** up to 2 tablespoons **honey** or corn syrup, ¼ teaspoon **ground cinnamon** (optional), and a few tablespoons **apple juice** or water, if needed to give purée the consistency of cake batter.

Pulpy apples. Core and slice **apples** to make about 2½ cups. Put in a 1½- to 2-quart pan with ⅓ cup **apple juice** or water. Simmer, covered, until soft when mashed (about 10 minutes). Let cool slightly. Purée with 1 tablespoon **lemon juice,** up to 2 tablespoons **honey** or corn syrup, ¼ teaspoon **ground cinnamon** (optional), and a few tablespoons **apple juice** or water, if needed to give purée the consistency of cake batter.

Apricot. Halve and pit **apricots** to make about 1½ cups. Purée with 1 tablespoon **lemon juice** and up to 3 tablespoons **honey** or corn syrup.

Cherry. Pit about 1½ cups **sweet cherries.** Purée with 1 tablespoon **lemon juice.**

Peach or nectarine. Halve, pit, and slice **peaches or nectarines** to make about 2 cups. Purée with 1 tablespoon **lemon juice** and up to 2 tablespoons **honey** or corn syrup.

Pear. Juicy Bartletts are best. Core and slice **pears** to make about 2 cups. Purée with 1 tablespoon **lemon juice.**

Plum. Cut flesh away from pits of **plums** to make about 1½ cups. Purée with 1 tablespoon **lemon juice** and about 2 tablespoons **honey** or corn syrup.

Raspberry or blackberry (including boysenberries, olallieberries, and loganberries; you may use a mixture of berries). Purée about 2 cups **berries** with 1 tablespoon **lemon juice** and up to ¼ cup **honey** or corn syrup. Press through a fine strainer; discard seeds.

Strawberry. Remove hulls from 1¼ to 1½ cups **strawberries.** Purée berries with 1 tablespoon **lemon juice** and up to 2 tablespoons **honey** or corn syrup.

Spiced Apple Rings

❤ ❤ ❤

Preparation time: 50 to 60 minutes, plus 1 week to stand
Storage time: Up to 1 year in a cool place

Cheery red color and spicy flavor make these apple rings appropriate for the Thanksgiving or Christmas holidays.

    6   cups sugar
    1⅔ cups cider vinegar
    1   teaspoon red food color (optional)
    4   cinnamon sticks (*each* about 3 inches long)
    2   teaspoons whole cloves
        About 4 pounds (about 12 medium-size) firm Golden Delicious apples, peeled and cored

Prepare four 1-pint canning jars as directed for Short-cook Jam (page 62).

Place sugar in a 5-quart pan along with vinegar, food color (if used), cinnamon sticks, and cloves. Bring mixture to a boil, uncovered; reduce heat and simmer for 10 minutes.

Slice apples crosswise into ⅓-inch-thick rings. Add to simmering syrup and cook, turning occasionally, until apples are barely tender when pierced and just becoming translucent around edges (6 to 8 minutes).

With a fork, lift apples from syrup; evenly fill prepared, hot jars. Leaving spices in pan, ladle enough hot syrup into jars to come within ½ inch of rims. Wipe rims clean; top with hot lids, then firmly screw on rings. Let cool on a towel, away from drafts. Test for seals as directed on page 62. Refrigerate any unsealed jars and use as soon as possible; store sealed jars in a cool place for at least 1 week or up to 1 year. Makes 4 pints.

Spiced Pineapple Spears

❤ ❤ ❤

Preparation time: About 1 hour
Storage time: Up to 1 year in a cool place

Fresh pineapple takes on the flavors of cardamom, allspice, cinnamon, and chiles in this unique and delicious preserve.

    3   medium-size pineapples (3 to 3½ lbs. *each*)
    1½ cups distilled white vinegar
    2   cups sugar
    2   tablespoons whole cloves
    1   tablespoon whole cardamom, lightly crushed
    1   teaspoon whole allspice
    3   cinnamon sticks (*each* about 3 inches long)
    1   small dried hot red chile, seeded

Peel and core pineapples, reserving as much juice as possible. Cut pineapple into 3-inch-long, ½-inch-thick spears. Set aside. Measure reserved pineapple juice; add enough water to make 1½ cups liquid. Set aside.

Prepare four 1-pint canning jars as directed for Short-cook Jam (page 62). Meanwhile, pour pineapple juice into a 6-quart pan; stir in vinegar, sugar, cloves, cardamom, allspice, cinnamon sticks, and chile. Bring to a boil over high heat; reduce heat, cover, and simmer for 15 minutes. Add half the pineapple spears; cover and simmer for 5 minutes.

With a fork, lift spears from syrup and fill 2 prepared, hot jars. Leaving spices in pan, ladle enough hot syrup into jars to come within ½ inch of rims. Wipe rims clean; top with hot lids, then firmly screw on rings.

Add remaining pineapple spears to syrup; cover and simmer for 5 minutes. Then fill remaining 2 jars as directed above. Let jars cool on a towel, away from drafts. Test for seals as directed on page 62. Refrigerate any unsealed jars and use as soon as possible; store sealed jars in a cool place for up to 1 year. Makes 4 pints.

Fresh Melon Pickles

❤ ❤ ❤

Preparation time: About 20 minutes, plus 2 hours to chill
Storage time: Up to 1 day in refrigerator

Capture the summery flavor of fresh melon with these no-cook pickles. They make a pretty and appealing last-minute gift.

    ½   cup white wine vinegar
    2   tablespoons sugar
    1   teaspoon *each* minced fresh tarragon, dill, and mint; or ½ teaspoon *each* dry tarragon, dill weed, and mint
    2   cups 1-inch melon cubes (Casaba, Santa Claus, green or orange honeydew, or Persian)

In a bowl, stir together vinegar, sugar, tarragon, dill, and mint until sugar is dissolved. Stir in melon. Cover and store in refrigerator for at least 2 hours or up to 1 day, stirring occasionally. Pack into glass jars for giving. Makes 2 cups.

Homegrown vegetables turn into real show-offs when
pickled and packed in attractive jars. Here (counterclockwise from front) are Marinated
Baby Carrots (facing page), Dilly Beans (facing page),
Refrigerator Corn Relish (page 76), New Mexico Marinated Peppers (facing page),
and Sweet Freezer Chips (page 81).

MARINATED BABY CARROTS

(Pictured on facing page)

♥ ♥ ♥

Preparation time: 25 to 30 minutes, plus at least 2 days to marinate
Storage time: Up to 3 weeks in refrigerator

Miniature carrots (sometimes called French carrots) or baby carrots are particularly appealing when lightly cooked, then marinated in a spicy, dill-seasoned vinegar-sugar mixture. Their petite size and inherent sweetness make them a snack that weight watchers will appreciate.

> About 1 pound baby carrots, peeled
> 2 bay leaves
> ½ cup distilled white vinegar
> ¼ cup water
> 3 tablespoons sugar
> ½ teaspoon *each* salt, mustard seeds, and dry dill weed
> ¼ teaspoon *each* crushed red pepper and dill seeds
> 1 clove garlic, minced or pressed

Arrange whole carrots in a vegetable steamer. Cover and steam over boiling water until just tender when pierced (10 to 12 minutes). Plunge into cold water to cool quickly; then drain.

Arrange carrots vertically in a clean 1-pint jar that is about the same height as carrots. Tuck in bay leaves. In a bowl, stir together vinegar, water, sugar, salt, mustard seeds, dill weed, red pepper, dill seeds, and garlic until sugar is dissolved. Pour over carrots, cover tightly, and refrigerate for at least 2 days or up to 3 weeks. Makes 1 pint.

DILLY BEANS

(Pictured on facing page)

♥ ♥ ♥

Preparation time: 30 to 45 minutes, plus at least 8 hours to marinate
Storage time: Up to 2 weeks in refrigerator

Take advantage of the harvest from your garden— or a good buy at the market—with this simple recipe. For an attractive effect, pack the seasoned beans vertically in pretty glass jars, as shown in the photo.

> 2 pounds green beans, ends removed
> 8 cups water
> 3 tablespoons coarse (kosher-style) salt
> 2 teaspoons *each* mustard seeds and dry dill weed

> 1 teaspoon *each* crushed red pepper and dill seeds
> 4 cloves garlic
> 2 cups *each* water and white wine vinegar
> ⅔ cup sugar

Leave beans whole (cut any extra-long beans in half). In a large pan, bring the 8 cups water to a boil; add beans and 1 tablespoon of the salt. Return to a boil and cook, uncovered, until beans are just tender-crisp to bite (about 5 minutes). Drain immediately and let cool. Pack beans into four 1-pint canning jars. Into each jar, put ½ teaspoon *each* mustard seeds and dill weed, ¼ teaspoon *each* red pepper and dill seeds, and 1 clove garlic.

In a pan, combine the 2 cups water, vinegar, sugar, and remaining 2 tablespoons salt. Bring to a boil. Pour ¼ of the mixture into each jar. Let cool. Cover jars tightly and store in refrigerator for at least 8 hours or up to 2 weeks. Makes 4 pints.

NEW MEXICO MARINATED PEPPERS

(Pictured on facing page)

♥ ♥ ♥

Preparation time: 25 to 30 minutes, plus 1 week to marinate
Storage time: Up to 1 month in refrigerator

Next time you attend a buffet or barbecue, take along this handsome relish as a gift for the hostess. Red or green bell peppers are layered with onion rings, then marinated in a garlicky pickling liquid.

> 6 large red or green bell peppers (or use 3 of each)
> 3 large cloves garlic, thinly sliced
> 1 cup *each* salad oil, white wine vinegar, and water
> 2 teaspoons sugar
> 4 teaspoons seasoned salt
> 1 teaspoon whole black peppercorns
> 2 medium-size onions, thinly sliced and separated into rings

Cut bell peppers in half; remove stems, seeds, and membranes. Then cut each pepper half lengthwise into ¾-inch-wide strips.

In a 5- to 6-quart pan, combine garlic, oil, vinegar, water, sugar, salt, and peppercorns. Bring to a boil over high heat; add bell pepper strips and boil gently, stirring, for 3 minutes. Remove from heat, stir in onions, and ladle into five 1-pint canning jars. Let cool, then cover tightly. Store in refrigerator for at least 1 week or up to 1 month. Makes 5 pints.

REFRIGERATOR CORN RELISH

(Pictured on page 74)

Preparation time: 30 to 45 minutes
Storage time: Up to 1 month in refrigerator

This good old-fashioned relish is still a favorite on frankfurters or alongside hamburgers or other meats. Our quick refrigerator version makes it easy to pack up a jarful for everyone on your gift list.

1¼ cups distilled white vinegar
¾ cup sugar
2½ teaspoons salt
1¼ teaspoons celery seeds
¾ teaspoon mustard seeds
½ teaspoon liquid hot pepper seasoning
8 cups fresh corn kernels, cut from about 10 large ears corn
1 small green bell pepper, seeded and chopped
1 small red bell pepper, seeded and chopped
3 green onions (including tops), chopped

In a 3- to 4-quart pan, combine vinegar, sugar, salt, celery seeds, mustard seeds, hot pepper seasoning, and corn. Bring to a simmer over medium heat. Simmer, uncovered, for 5 minutes; then remove from heat and let cool.

Stir in bell peppers and onions. Pack into four 1-pint canning jars; cover tightly and store in refrigerator for up to 1 month. Makes about 4 pints.

PETER PIPER'S PEPPER PICKLES

Preparation time: 20 to 30 minutes, plus at least 1 day to marinate
Storage time: Up to 2 weeks in refrigerator

If your friends have a taste for hot and spicy foods, why not present them with a jar of fiery pickled chiles? You can use any type of chile in this recipe, from mild Anaheims to burning jalapeños.

To make 4 cups, you'll need about 5 cups **chiles** (any variety). Wearing rubber gloves, wash all chiles. Cut 2 small slits in each small chile (Fresno, jalapeño, serrano, yellow wax). Cut large chiles

(Anaheim, Hungarian hot wax, pasilla) into 2-inch lengths; remove seeds, if desired. Cook chiles in **boiling water** to cover until barely tender when pierced (5 to 7 minutes). Drain well. Pack in a wide-mouth quart jar with 1 clove **garlic.** Combine 1 cup *each* **distilled white vinegar** and **sugar** and ½ teaspoon **salt;** stir until sugar is dissolved. Pour over chiles to cover. Cover jar tightly and shake well; refrigerate for at least 1 day or up to 2 weeks. Pack into small glass jars for giving. Makes 4 cups.

GARDEN MARINARA SAUCE

(Pictured on page 79)

Preparation time: 1¼ to 1½ hours
Storage time: Up to 1 week in refrigerator; up to 6 months in freezer

When you give a jar of made-from-scratch marinara sauce, you're giving your lucky friends a head start on a great dinner—they need only add pasta, bread, and wine. (You might even include all the meal fixings in a basket, as shown on page 90.) Our sauce also goes into two classic Italian appetizer relishes—Caponata and Peperonata (both on page 78).

6 pounds (15 to 18 medium-size) fresh ripe tomatoes or 4 large cans (28 oz. *each*) whole tomatoes, drained
¼ cup olive oil
3 large onions, coarsely chopped
3 or 4 cloves garlic, minced or pressed
1 cup lightly packed fresh basil leaves, chopped
½ to 1 tablespoon sugar
 Salt and pepper

Dip fresh tomatoes in boiling water to cover for 10 seconds; core and peel. Chop fresh or canned tomatoes with a food processor or a knife.

Pour oil into a 12- to 14-inch frying pan; add onions and garlic and cook over medium heat, stirring frequently, until onions are golden brown (about 20 minutes). Add chopped tomatoes and basil. Cook, uncovered, stirring occasionally to prevent sticking, until sauce is reduced to 8 cups (45 to 60 minutes). Add sugar; season to taste with salt and pepper.

Ladle sauce into four 1-pint canning jars or freezer containers, leaving 1 inch headspace. Cover tightly; store in refrigerator for up to 1 week, in freezer for up to 6 months. Makes 4 pints.

Creating Your Own Labels & Tags

Labels and tags you create yourself add a personal touch that makes your homemade gift that much more special. Throughout this book, you'll see a number of appealing ideas for decorating handmade labels and tags. Below, we give simple instructions for the techniques used to create them—stenciling, stamping, and adding stickers or cutouts.

BASIC LABELS & TAGS

You can purchase plain tags and adhesive labels for decorating at stationery stores, card shops, and office supply stores. It's easy to make your own, too—just cut them from sheets of heavy or adhesive-backed paper (sold at art supply stores), making just the sizes and shapes you wish. For example, you might want to make some extra-large tags with space for writing out storage and/or serving instructions.

If you plan to make several tags, draw a pattern, trace around it onto the paper, and cut out with scissors; make a hole at one end with a hole punch, then thread with a loop of twine, silk cord, or narrow ribbon.

If you want to go one step further, you can glue your tag onto a stiffened fabric backing coordinated to match a fabric- or napkin-lined basket or a fabric-topped jar (see pages 30–31).

DECORATIONS

To decorate your labels and tags, use stenciling or stamping techniques (following). Or simply affix purchased stickers—apples, rainbows, or almost anything else you can name! You might also cut out motifs from a favorite wrapping paper or greeting card (use small, sharp scissors) and glue them to the label or tag.

To stencil, you'll need acrylic artist's paints, a stiff-bristled, flat-tipped stencil brush, a styrofoam meat tray or egg carton to use as a palette, a small piece of smooth, heavy cardboard, masking tape, and purchased stencil patterns. The patterns can be found in art or craft stores and in some fabric and needlework shops. They come in a variety of designs, from letters of the alphabet to flower patterns to decorative borders; be sure you choose a miniature motif that will fit nicely onto your tag or label.

To apply the stencil, lay the tag on the cardboard, then carefully position and tape the stencil

To make a stamp (top), *carve a cut raw potato using a craft knife. Apply a stencil* (bottom) *using a flat-tipped stencil brush.*

over it. Place a supply of paint on your styrofoam palette. Dip your stencil brush lightly in the paint, so only the flat ends of the bristles pick up paint. To remove excess paint, tap the brush lightly on a clean area of the palette (the brush should be fairly dry). Then dab the brush all over the area to be painted, using a straight-up-and-down motion. Be sure to cover the area (and edges) thoroughly. Remove the stencil; let the paint dry completely.

To stamp, you can use purchased rubber stamps, available in a wide array of designs, and inked stamp pads (these come in a range of colors, as well as the usual black). Or you can create your own stamp using a potato or a rubber art eraser.

To make a potato stamp, slice off the end of a raw potato (you could also use a turnip or rutabaga) to provide a smooth printing surface. Sketch the motif on the cut surface with a fine-tipped felt pen, keeping in mind that simple motifs—such as hearts, diamonds, and stars—work best. Remember that your stamp will print the *reverse* of the design as it appears on the vegetable. Using a sharp craft knife, cut away around the motif to a depth of about ¼ inch.

Ink the vegetable's cut surface on a stamp pad, then just stamp your labels and tags with one firm, even application. If you plan to save the vegetable for a second printing session in a few days, wrap and refrigerate it.

To make a more permanent stamp from a rubber art eraser, follow the same basic procedure as for the potato stamp; ink the eraser on a stamp pad to use.

Caponata

(Pictured on facing page)

♥ ♥ ♥

Preparation time: 45 to 50 minutes
Storage time: Up to 1 week in refrigerator; up to 6 months in freezer

Peppers, olives, and creamy-textured eggplant combine with homemade marinara sauce in this Italian relish. You might make it part of an "antipasto kit," along with other relishes, cheeses, and salami. Or give it on its own, as a dip for pocket bread or butter lettuce leaves.

    1½ pounds eggplant
    ½   cup olive oil
    2   large red or green bell peppers, seeded
        and diced
    1   large onion, chopped
    1   clove garlic, minced or pressed
    2½ cups Garden Marinara Sauce (page 76)
    1   cup sliced Spanish-style pimento-stuffed
        olives or sliced pitted ripe olives
        Salt and pepper

Cut unpeeled eggplant into ½-inch cubes. Pour oil into a 12- to 14-inch frying pan. Add eggplant; cover and cook over medium heat, stirring occasionally, until eggplant softens slightly (about 5 minutes). Uncover and continue to cook, stirring, until eggplant is browned (10 to 15 more minutes). Add bell peppers, onion, and garlic; stir until onion is soft. Add Garden Marinara Sauce; continue to cook, uncovered, until a thick sauce forms (about 10 more minutes). Add olives; season to taste with salt and pepper. Let cool to room temperature, then pack into four 1-pint canning jars or freezer containers, leaving 1 inch headspace. Cover tightly; store in refrigerator for up to 1 week, in freezer for up to 6 months. On gift tag, note that caponata may be served cold or at room temperature. Makes about 4 pints.

Peperonata

(Pictured on facing page)

♥ ♥ ♥

Preparation time: 30 to 40 minutes
Storage time: Up to 1 week in refrigerator; up to 6 months in freezer

This classic Italian appetizer relish—a colorful blend of sweet red, green, and yellow peppers—is based on our Garden Marinara Sauce. It's a good meat relish and a tasty dip for butter lettuce leaves and crackers.

        About 10 assorted red, green, and yellow
        bell peppers, seeded
    ¼   cup olive oil
    2   large onions, cut into 1-inch pieces,
        layers separated
    2   cloves garlic, minced or pressed
    2½ cups Garden Marinara Sauce (page 76)
        Salt and pepper

Cut peppers into thin slices with a food processor or a knife; you need 8 cups.

Pour oil into a 12- to 14-inch frying pan. Add onions and stir over medium heat, uncovered, for 3 minutes. Add peppers, garlic, and Garden Marinara Sauce; cover and cook until peppers are tender when pierced (8 to 10 minutes). Season to taste with salt and pepper.

Let cool to room temperature, then pack into four 1-pint canning jars or freezer containers, leaving 1 inch headspace. Cover tightly; store in refrigerator for up to 1 week, in freezer for up to 6 months. On gift tag, note that peperonata may be served cold or at room temperature. Makes about 4 pints.

Pickle-packed Beets

♥ ♥ ♥

Preparation time: About 1 hour, plus at least 1 day to marinate
Storage time: Up to 3 months in refrigerator

Onion slices and purple-red beets marinated in vinegar and sugar look festive in a glass jar—and taste delicious as a side dish or in a green salad.

    6 to 8 medium-size beets (about 2 lbs.
        total)
    1   medium-size mild white onion, thinly
        sliced
    1   cup distilled white vinegar
    ⅔   cup sugar
    1   clove garlic, minced or pressed (optional)

Scrub beets well, but do not peel; leave roots, stems, and skins intact to prevent "bleeding" during cooking. Place beets in a 4- to 5-quart pan and add water to cover. Bring to a boil; cover and boil until tender throughout when pierced (20 to 45 minutes). Drain beets and let cool; trim off roots and stems and slip off skins under cold running water. Cut beets into ¼-inch-thick slices.

Firmly pack beets and onion in alternating layers in two 1-pint canning jars. Combine vinegar, sugar, and garlic (if used); stir until sugar is dissolved, then pour over beets and onion to fill jars. Cover tightly; shake jars well. Store in refrigerator for at least 1 day or up to 3 months. Makes 2 pints.

The unbeatable flavors of sweet, red-ripe tomatoes
and heady fresh basil make our Garden Marinara Sauce (page 76) a sure-fire success.
Give the sauce (center) plain, to serve with pasta; or
use it in our colorful Caponata (back) and Peperonata (front). (The recipes are on
the facing page.)

Packing & Sending Your Gifts

Sending homemade food to family and friends far away takes a little extra planning and care, but the effort is repaid in the recipient's delight at a very special gift. To make sure the foods you send arrive in good shape, follow the suggestions below.

FOODS TO MAIL

Generally, it's best not to mail highly perishable foods such as pâtés, meats, and cheeses; there's just no guarantee against spoilage. Instead, choose baked goods, candies, or preserves.

Cookies should be sturdy and firm. Avoid fragile and sticky cookies and those with moist frostings. Crisp cookies are fine if they're not too delicate and crumbly, but the most reliable travelers are cookies that are slightly soft, yet firm: oatmeal cookies and brownies, for example.

Unfrosted, firm-textured cakes, such as pound cakes and fruitcakes, are good choices for mailing; stay away from delicate cakes and those with perishable fillings. Firm, unfrosted quick breads travel well, too.

Of course, all baked goods must be fresh when you send them, and must be packaged properly.

Some candies, such as fruit-nut types, fudge, and hard candies, are good travelers, provided they aren't too sticky. Chocolate candy requires special handling, however. You should send it by overnight express mail—and probably not at all in the hot summer months. Among the best goodies to mail are candied popcorn and flavored nuts.

Most homemade jams, jellies, relishes, and other preserves are acceptable for mailing, provided the jars are securely sealed and carefully cushioned (see below). Liquids, such as flavored vinegars and oils or syrups, are riskier. They must be in tightly sealed bottles with screw caps and should be specially packed as described below. Note that it's illegal to send alcoholic beverages by U.S. mail or to ship them across state lines by private carrier.

PACKING & CUSHIONING GIFTS

To send food safely through the mail, wrap it airtight for freshness, package it securely in a small container such as a box or tin, and pack that container, surrounded by padding on all sides, in a larger corrugated fiberboard shipping box.

Cookies can be layered in tins, sturdy foil-lined boxes, rigid plastic containers, or foil loaf or pie pans; you may want to wrap small stacks of cookies in foil before packing them. (Be sure to pack soft and crisp cookies separately to preserve their textures.) Separate layers with wax paper or plastic bubble wrap, and pack the cookies securely so they won't jostle about and damage each other in transit. Candies can be sent the same way, though it's a good idea to separate small candies in bonbon cups before packing them. If you're packing the cookies or candy in a box that isn't airtight, seal it in a plastic bag.

Cakes can be packed in snug-fitting, tight-lidded tins. You can also bake cakes (and quick breads) in disposable foil pans, then send them right in the pan, wrapped tightly in plastic or heat-sealed (see page 30).

Pack an individual jar or bottle in a sturdy box, surrounded with enough absorbent cushioning to soak up the entire contents. Effective absorbent materials include cotton padding, pulverized paper (not to be confused with shredded paper), and blotting paper. If you're sending more than one jar, pack the jars in a box with cardboard dividers and cushion as described above.

PACKING THE SHIPPING BOX

Once you have the inner box or tin packed and firmly closed, you're ready to pack it into a sturdy shipping carton. If you're sending several items in the same carton, make sure the boxes are separated, and pack heavier items beneath lighter ones.

Pad the bottom of the shipping box with popcorn, polystyrene pellets, or wadded or shredded newspaper. Pack the smaller box or boxes into the large box, padding well on all sides and between containers. Finally, add padding over the top of everything, then shake the box to make sure there's no jostling. Slip in an extra address label in case the outer label is damaged, then seal the box thoroughly with wide reinforced kraft paper tape or filament (strapping) tape. Label clearly, then cover the label with transparent tape so rain can't smear the ink. Ship your goodies first class so they'll reach their destination quickly.

ZUCCHINI PICKLES

♥ ♥ ♥

Preparation time: 35 to 40 minutes, plus 1 to 2 hours to stand
Storage time: Up to 3 months in refrigerator

If your garden runneth over with zucchini, try these easy pickles. They taste much like the familiar bread-and-butter pickles.

    5 pounds medium-size zucchini
    2 pounds mild white onions, thinly sliced
    ¼ cup salt
       Ice water
    4 cups cider vinegar
    2 cups sugar
    1 tablespoon *each* celery seeds and ground turmeric
    2 tablespoons mustard seeds
    2 teaspoons ground ginger
    3 cloves garlic, minced or pressed

Cut zucchini into ¼-inch-thick slices. Place zucchini, onions, and salt in a large bowl; cover with ice water and let stand at room temperature for 1 to 2 hours. Drain, rinse well, and drain again.

In a 10- to 12-quart pan, combine vinegar, sugar, celery seeds, turmeric, mustard seeds, ginger, and garlic. Bring to a boil over high heat, stirring to dissolve sugar. Boil, uncovered, for 2 to 3 minutes; stir in zucchini mixture, return to a boil, and boil for 2 more minutes.

Pack pickles into eight 1-pint canning jars, leaving ¼ inch headspace. Cover tightly; let cool. Store in refrigerator for up to 3 months. Makes 8 pints.

SWEET FREEZER CHIPS

(Pictured on page 74)

♥ ♥ ♥

Preparation time: 30 to 40 minutes, plus 2 to 3 hours to marinate,
1 week to mellow in freezer
Storage time: Up to 6 months in freezer

Nothing could be easier to prepare than these fresh-tasting pickles. You just layer sliced cucumbers and onions in jars and freeze them in a vinegar and sugar syrup.

    1   medium-size mild white onion
    2½ pounds (about 5 medium-size) cucumbers
    2   tablespoons salt

    8 cups ice cubes
    4 cups sugar
    2 cups cider vinegar

Thinly slice onion; cut unpeeled cucumbers into ⅛-inch-thick slices. Mix cucumbers, onion, and salt in a large bowl; cover mixture with ice cubes and refrigerate for 2 to 3 hours.

Drain off water and discard unmelted ice cubes; do not rinse vegetables. Pack cucumber and onion slices into three 1-pint freezer containers or canning jars, leaving 1½ inches headspace.

In a 2-quart pan, combine sugar and vinegar; bring to a boil, stirring until sugar is dissolved. Pour just enough hot syrup over cucumbers to cover. Cover containers; let cool, then store in freezer for at least 1 week or up to 6 months. To thaw, place containers in refrigerator for at least 8 hours. Makes about 3 pints.

QUICK REFRIGERATOR CUCUMBER CHIPS

♥ ♥ ♥

Preparation time: About 30 minutes, plus 1 to 2 hours to marinate,
24 hours to chill
Storage time: Up to 3 weeks in refrigerator

Brightened with strips of red bell pepper, these simple sweet pickles require no cooking.

    3   large regular cucumbers or 2 long thin-skinned (English or Armenian) cucumbers
    1   large red bell pepper, seeded and cut lengthwise into ½-inch-wide strips
    1   medium-size onion, thinly sliced
    1   tablespoon salt
    2   teaspoons dill seeds
    ¾   cup sugar
    ½   cup white wine vinegar

Cut unpeeled cucumbers into ¹⁄₁₆-inch-thick slices; you should have about 6 cups. In a large bowl, combine cucumbers, bell pepper, and onion. Sprinkle with salt and dill seeds; then stir well. Let stand, uncovered, for 1 to 2 hours, stirring occasionally.

Combine sugar and vinegar and stir until sugar is dissolved, then pour over vegetables and mix gently. Ladle mixture into four 1-pint canning jars. Cover tightly and store in refrigerator for at least 24 hours or up to 3 weeks. Makes about 4 pints.

Within the photo, handwritten labels read:

Spiced German Mustard

French Old-Fashioned Mustard

Recipe *Mustard Vinaigrette*   Serves *1 Cup*

Packed in good-looking crocks or plump glass jars,
homemade mustards (facing page) are sure to win approval from the cooks on your list.
We offer crunchy French and German styles, as well
as smooth Dijon mustard with two flavor variations. Include your favorite mustard
vinaigrette recipe on the gift tag.

Mustards—Spicy to Mild

Though mustard in dozens of varieties is easy to find at your local gourmet shop, it's fun and easy to make at home. Using our recipes, you can produce a velvety-smooth or crunchy, coarse mustard, a mellow spread or one that's hot and pungent.

For coarse-grained mustard, use whole seeds; for a smooth product, use dry mustard (you can buy both in bulk from spice shops).

Mustard is hottest when freshly made, mellower as it ages. If you want to give a really hot version, don't make it too far in advance; if you prefer milder mustard, let it age.

In our recipes, an infusion of vinegar, wine, and spices adds flavor and dilutes the basic mustard-water paste. The concentration of this mixture also affects the mustard's pungency. When the infusion is reduced by half, the resulting mustard is medium-hot. But cooking tempers mustard's hotness: if you want a very hot mustard, use a more reduced infusion so the mustard will need less cooking to thicken.

DIJON-STYLE MUSTARD

Smoothly stir ½ cup **cold water** into 1 cup **dry mustard;** let stand for at least 10 minutes.

In a 2- to 3-quart noncorrodible pan, combine 1⅓ cups *each* **dry white wine** and **white wine vinegar;** 1 small **onion,** chopped, or ½ cup chopped shallots; 3 large cloves **garlic,** pressed or minced; 2 **bay leaves;** 8 **whole allspice;** 2 teaspoons *each* **salt** and **sugar;**

and 1 teaspoon **dry tarragon.** Bring to a boil; boil, uncovered, until reduced by half (15 to 20 minutes).

Pour wine mixture through a wire strainer into mustard paste, pressing all juices out. Stir to blend; pour into top of a double boiler over simmering water. Cook, stirring occasionally, until as thick as very heavy cream (10 to 15 minutes; mixture thickens slightly more as it cools). Let cool, pack into small jars or crocks, and cover tightly. Store in refrigerator for up to 2 years. Makes 2 cups.

HONEY DIJON MUSTARD. Follow directions for **Dijon-style Mustard,** but omit dry tarragon. After cooking, stir in ¼ cup *each* **dark corn syrup** and **honey.**

GREEN PEPPERCORN DIJON MUSTARD. Follow directions for **Dijon-style Mustard,** but stir 2 tablespoons minced **green peppercorns** into mustard after cooking.

FRENCH OLD-FASHIONED MUSTARD

Soak ½ cup **white mustard seeds** and 1 tablespoon **dry mustard** in ½ cup **cold water** for 3 hours.

In a 1- to 2-quart noncorrodible pan, combine ½ cup *each* **white wine vinegar** and **dry white wine;** 1 small **onion,** chopped, or ½ cup chopped shallots; 2 cloves **garlic,** pressed or minced; 1 teaspoon *each* **salt** and **sugar;** ½ teaspoon **dry tarragon;** 1 **bay leaf;** and ⅛ teaspoon *each* **ground allspice** and **ground turmeric.** Simmer, uncovered, over

medium heat until reduced by half (10 to 15 minutes). Pour liquid through a wire strainer into mustard seed mixture; whirl in a blender until coarsely ground. Cook in the top of a double boiler over simmering water, stirring occasionally, until thickened (8 to 12 minutes). Let cool, pack into a jar or crock, and cover tightly. Store in refrigerator for at least 3 days or up to 2 years. Makes about 1 cup.

SPICED GERMAN MUSTARD

Soak ⅓ cup **white mustard seeds** and ¼ cup **dry mustard** in ½ cup **cold water** for 3 hours.

In a 1- to 2-quart noncorrodible pan, combine 1 cup **cider vinegar;** 1 small **onion,** chopped; 2 tablespoons firmly packed **brown sugar;** 1 teaspoon **salt;** 2 cloves **garlic,** pressed or minced; ½ teaspoon **ground cinnamon;** ¼ teaspoon *each* **ground allspice, dill seeds,** and **dry tarragon;** and ⅛ teaspoon **ground turmeric.** Simmer, uncovered, over medium heat until reduced by about half (10 to 15 minutes). Pour liquid through a wire strainer into mustard seed mixture; whirl in a blender or food processor until pureéd to the texture you like. Cook in the top of a double boiler over simmering water, stirring occasionally, until thickened (10 to 15 minutes; mustard thickens slightly more as it cools). Stir in 1 to 2 tablespoons **honey.** Let cool, pack into a jar or crock, and cover tightly. Store in refrigerator for at least 3 days or up to 2 years. Makes about 1 cup.

SPICY SEVEN-DAY PICKLES

♥ ♥ ♥

Preparation time: About 30 minutes, plus 1 week to stand and chill
Storage time: Up to 3 months in refrigerator

Follow the easy steps in this recipe, and at the end of a week you'll have pickles! These have an agreeably spicy-sweet taste (similar to pickled watermelon rind) that's sure to please anybody who likes relishes.

- **3½ pounds (about 7 medium-size) cucumbers**
- **4 cups sugar**
- **2 cups distilled white vinegar**
- **1 tablespoon whole mixed pickling spice**
- **2 teaspoons salt**

Place unpeeled cucumbers in a deep bowl, cover with boiling water, and let stand until next day. Then drain cucumbers, cover again with boiling water, and let stand until next day. Repeat this procedure on the third and fourth days.

On the fifth day, drain cucumbers, then cut into ¼-inch-thick slices. Place sliced cucumbers in a clean, deep bowl.

In a 3-quart pan, combine sugar, vinegar, pickling spice, and salt. Bring to a boil, stirring to dissolve sugar; pour over cucumbers. Let cool, then cover and refrigerate for 2 days.

On the seventh day, bring cucumber mixture to a boil. Pack into five 1-pint canning jars, leaving ¼ inch headspace. Cover tightly; let cool. Store in refrigerator for up to 3 months. Makes 5 pints.

SWEET-SOUR ORANGE PICKLES

♥ ♥ ♥

Preparation time: 45 to 50 minutes
Storage time: Up to 3 weeks in refrigerator

Take advantage of your microwave oven to make tangy, fragrant pickles from fresh oranges. Dotted with currants, they're an unusual accompaniment for meats or poultry. If you wish, you can substitute thin-skinned tangerines for the oranges.

- **2 medium-size thin-skinned oranges (such as Valencia), ends trimmed**
- **1½ cups water**

- **2 cinnamon sticks (*each* about 3 inches long)**
- **¼ teaspoon *each* salt, ground allspice, and ground nutmeg**
- **½ teaspoon ground ginger**
- **⅓ cup *each* sugar and currants**
- **⅔ cup cider vinegar**
- **¼ to ½ teaspoon crushed dried hot red chiles**

Wash oranges and cut in half lengthwise, then thinly slice crosswise. Discard any seeds. Place oranges and water in a deep nonmetallic bowl. Cover with plastic wrap and microwave on full power, stirring every 5 minutes, until peel is tender when pierced (12 to 15 minutes). Protect hands from heat when stirring.

Drain oranges, discarding liquid. Stir in cinnamon sticks, salt, allspice, nutmeg, ginger, sugar, currants, vinegar, and chiles. Cover with plastic wrap and microwave on full power, stirring every 4 minutes, until orange peel is very tender when pierced and almost all liquid has evaporated (16 to 20 minutes). Let cool; cover and store in refrigerator for up to 3 weeks. Pack into glass jars for giving; on gift tag, note that pickles may be served chilled or at room temperature. Makes about 2 cups.

♥ SWEET-SOUR TANGERINE PICKLES

Follow directions for **Sweet-Sour Orange Pickles,** but use 3 medium-size thin-skinned **tangerines** instead of oranges. Makes about 1½ cups.

MEXICAN-STYLE SALSA

Preparation time: About 2½ hours
Storage time: Up to 1 week in refrigerator; up to 6 months in freezer

Salsa made with fresh tomatoes and chiles is the soul of Mexican cookery. To adjust the heat of this classic salsa recipe, simply add more or fewer chiles. On the gift tag, suggest using the salsa as a condiment for barbecued meats or poultry, scrambled eggs, or any Mexican-style dish.

- **5 pounds (about 10 large) firm-ripe tomatoes**
- **1 large onion, coarsely chopped**

12 to 18 fresh jalapeño or Fresno chiles (⅓ to
   ½ lb. *total*), seeded and finely minced
16 to 21 fresh serrano chiles (about 3 oz.
   total), seeded and finely minced
 1 tablespoon minced or pressed garlic
 ¼ cup cider vinegar
 1 teaspoon salt
 ½ teaspoon pepper

Core and coarsely chop tomatoes. Put tomatoes and their juice, along with onion, in a 6- to 8-quart pan. Stir in chiles, garlic, vinegar, salt, and pepper. Bring to a boil over high heat. Reduce heat and boil gently, uncovered, stirring occasionally, until salsa is reduced to 7 cups (about 2 hours); as salsa thickens, stir more often to prevent sticking.

Let cool, then ladle into ½- to 1-cup canning jars or freezer containers, leaving 1 inch headspace. Cover tightly; store in refrigerator for up to 1 week, in freezer for up to 6 months. Makes 7 cups.

SOUTHWESTERN RED CHILE SAUCE

Preparation time: 45 to 60 minutes
Storage time: Up to 1 week in refrigerator; up to 6 months in freezer

First toasted, then simmered and puréed, dried red chiles make a sauce with an extra-rich flavor. On the gift tag, suggest using the sauce alone on cheese omelets; mixing it with mayonnaise or sour cream to make a dip for seafood; or using it as the base for other southwestern-style sauces (enchilada sauce, for example).

 3 ounces (about 9) dried red New Mexico
   or California chiles
2½ cups water
 1 small onion, cut into chunks
 2 cloves garlic
   Salt

Wipe dust off chiles and lay them on a 12- by 15-inch baking sheet. Bake in a 450° oven just until chiles smell toasted (2 to 3 minutes). Let cool; break off stems, then shake out and discard seeds.

In a 3- to 4-quart pan, combine chiles, water, onion, and garlic. Cover and bring to a boil over high heat. Reduce heat and simmer until chiles are very soft when pierced (about 30 minutes). Remove from heat and let cool slightly, then whirl in a blender until very smoothly puréed.

Rub purée firmly through a wire strainer to extract all pulp; discard residue. Season to taste with salt. Spoon sauce into three ½-pint canning jars or freezer containers, leaving 1 inch headspace. Cover tightly; store in refrigerator for up to 1 week, in freezer for up to 6 months. Makes about 3 cups.

MILD CHILE SAUCE

Preparation time: About 2½ hours
Storage time: Up to 1 year in a cool place

In this recipe, mild green Anaheim chiles add just a suggestion of heat to a tomato-onion sauce seasoned with sweet spices. It's a great topping for barbecued hamburgers, chicken, or even scrambled eggs.

 7 pounds (about 14 large) ripe tomatoes,
   quartered
 4 large fresh green chiles (such as
   Anaheim, California, or pasilla), seeded
   (if desired) and chopped
 2 large onions, quartered
 2 cloves garlic
1½ cups sugar
 2 tablespoons salt
 3 cups cider vinegar
1½ teaspoons *each* ground cinnamon and
   cloves
 1 teaspoon ground ginger

In a large bowl, combine tomatoes, chiles, onions, and garlic. Whirl in a blender or food processor, a portion at a time, until smooth. Pour into an 8-quart pan and stir in sugar, salt, vinegar, cinnamon, cloves, and ginger. Cook over medium-high heat, uncovered, until thickened and reduced to 8 cups (about 2 hours), stirring frequently; as sauce thickens, reduce heat and stir more often to prevent sticking.

While sauce simmers, prepare four 1-pint canning jars as directed for Short-cook Jam (page 62).

Fill prepared, hot jars with hot sauce to within ¼ inch of rims. Run a rubber spatula or blunt knife down between sauce and sides of jars to release air bubbles. Wipe rims clean; top with hot lids, then firmly screw on rings.

Process jars of sauce as directed for Short-cook Jam (page 62). Let cool on a towel, away from drafts. Test for seals as directed on page 62. Refrigerate any unsealed jars and use as soon as possible; store sealed jars in a cool place for up to 1 year. Makes 4 pints.

Distinctive Vinegars & Oils

Among the most beautiful and special gifts to emerge from the kitchen, these vinegars and oils, aromatic with fresh herbs, whole spices, and chiles, are both easy and inexpensive to make.

FLAVORING WINE VINEGARS

Use your imagination in creating flavorings for wine vinegars; we suggest just a few seasonings and combinations of herbs below. Be sure to begin the process well in advance, since you'll need to let the vinegar stand for several weeks to absorb the flavors.

Give the vinegars in decorative bottles (3- to 3½-cup size). Any bottle you choose should have a tight-fitting screw top, stopper, or cork. Put the spices or rinsed herbs of your choice in the clean bottle, then fill with plain wine vinegar. Leave an inch free at the top if you plan to insert a cork or glass stopper. Let the bottles stand undisturbed in a cool, dark place for at least 3 weeks so flavors can develop. The vinegars keep well for about 4 months.

Each of our recipes makes about 3½ cups vinegar.

GARLIC-LEMON-MINT VINEGAR

Put into a bottle 4 large cloves **garlic** (peeled) and 4 **fresh mint sprigs** (*each* about 5 inches long). Add a ¼-inch-wide strip of **lemon peel** (cut in a continuous spiral). Fill with **white wine vinegar.**

GARLIC VINEGAR

Peel 6 large cloves **garlic** and impale them on a thin bamboo skewer (or put 3 garlic cloves on each of 2 skewers). Insert in a bottle and fill with **red wine vinegar.**

TARRAGON OR DILL VINEGAR

Poke 4 **fresh tarragon or dill sprigs** (*each* about 5 inches long) into a bottle. Fill with **red or white wine vinegar.**

SPICY CHILE VINEGAR

Poke into a bottle 4 **bay leaves,** 6 **small dried hot red chiles,** and 4 large cloves **garlic** (peeled). Fill with **red or white wine vinegar.**

FLAVORING OILS

Herbs and spices quickly add pleasing flavors to olive oil or neutral-tasting salad oil.

Fresh herbs will cloud the oil as they decompose, so it's best to give and use these oils as soon as the flavors develop (it takes about a week). If oils do become cloudy, strain them into another container.

Note: Since fresh basil turns black in oil, we do not recommend its use here. If you want to include garlic, spear peeled cloves on a skewer as for Garlic Vinegar, above; remove if garlic develops a fuzzy haze.

Fill and cap decorative bottles as for vinegars; store in a cool, dark place for at least 7 days so flavors can develop. Oils will keep for 2 to 3 months.

DILL OIL

Push 2 or 3 large **seed heads of fresh dill,** stems first, into a 1- to 3-cup narrow-necked bottle. Fill with **olive oil** (extra-virgin, if desired) or salad oil.

FRESH GREEN HERBS OIL

In a 1- to 3-cup narrow-necked bottle, put 4 to 6 sprigs *each* **fresh thyme, fresh tarragon, fresh rosemary,** and **fresh sage;** all herb sprigs should be 5 to 6 inches long. Also add 2 **fresh or dry bay leaves** and 1 teaspoon **whole black peppercorns.** Fill with **olive oil** (extra-virgin, if desired) or salad oil.

SOLO HERB OIL

Follow directions for **Fresh Green Herbs Oil,** but use any one of the **herbs** alone in a 1- to 1½-cup bottle with **olive oil** (extra-virgin, if desired) or salad oil and 1 teaspoon **whole black peppercorns.**

GINGER-SPICE OIL

To 1 to 2 cups **salad oil,** add 2 or 3 thin, quarter-size slices **fresh ginger,** 1 **cinnamon stick** (3 to 4 inches long), 3 or 4 **small dried hot red chiles,** and 1 teaspoon *each* lightly crushed **coriander seeds** and lightly crushed **cumin seeds.**

Aromatic fresh herb sprigs, a dash of spice, hot
chiles, a spear of garlic cloves—these simple ingredients turn ordinary wine vinegar,
salad oil, and olive oil into unique culinary gifts.
Present the salad makers in tall glass bottles sealed with corks. (The recipes are on the
facing page.)

MADE-TO-ORDER GIFT BASKETS

Bountiful offerings for all occasions

For a very special occasion or simply when you're in the mood to splurge, why not put together a whole collection of goodies? In this chapter, we present four ideas for gift baskets of food and accessories, each with a theme. Choose an elegant afternoon tea, a complete Italian pasta dinner, a lavish spread for a picnic, or a winter-warmer dessert buffet.

We've filled each basket with one or two specialty items (recipes given here) plus an assortment of treats from other chapters in this book, but you can substitute purchased foods for some of these if you prefer. For example, you might make only the salami for the picnic meal, then buy a loaf of dark bread and jars of mustard and pickles. And of course, you may want to use other favorite items in place of those we've suggested. The fun is in dreaming up just the right combination for the person you have in mind!

TEATIME BASKET

Few customs are more delightful or delicious than the traditional British afternoon tea. It's a sociable ritual where cups of steaming-hot, freshly brewed tea—complete with milk, sugar, and lemon—are passed around with assorted cookies and cakes, and tender scones slathered with sweet jam or tangy lemon curd.

The makings for our American version of a British tea party are an ideal gift for any tea lover with a sweet tooth. Choose an assortment of black teas such as Ceylon, Darjeeling, and English or Irish Breakfast; or give one black tea plus one or more of our special tea blends—minted citrus, spicy orange, or mint. For baked goodies, offer Brown Sugar Shortbreads or Scottish Ecclefechan Raisin Tart (or both) and scones with homemade jam and lemon curd.

Package the teas in individual little tins, the baked goods in larger tins. Arrange these, along with jars of jam and lemon curd, in a basket lined with a lacy white or pastel napkin. If you wish, tuck in a little china teapot and a tea infuser.

♥

**Spicy Orange, Cool Mint,
or Minted Citrus Tea Blend (recipes follow)
Classic Black Tea of Your Choice
Buttermilk Scone Hearts (page 19)
Fruit Jam of Your Choice (page 62)
Quick Lemon or Lime Curd (page 68)
Brown Sugar Shortbreads (page 49)
or
Ecclefechan Raisin Tart (recipe follows)**

♥

TEA BLENDS

For all three tea blends below, attach a gift tag with these brewing directions: To brew tea, for each serving place 1 teaspoon tea in a tea infuser. Add ¾ cup boiling water for each serving. Steep for 2 to 4 minutes or until tea is as strong as you like.

All teas can be served with sugar; for Spicy Orange Tea Blend, you might also suggest offering orange wedges to squeeze into each cup.

Spicy Orange Tea Blend. Using a mortar and pestle, crush 2½ tablespoons **whole cloves** and 5 **cinnamon sticks** (*each* 3 inches long) until partly broken. Mix with ¼ pound **orange pekoe tea blend,** ¼ cup *each* **dried orange peel** and finely chopped **crystallized ginger,** and 1 teaspoon **ground nutmeg.**

Cool Mint Tea Blend. Mix ¼ pound **Darjeeling or orange pekoe tea blend** and ¾ ounce (about ¼ cup) **peppermint or spearmint tea.**

Minted Citrus Tea Blend. Mix ½ pound **orange pekoe tea blend,** 2 tablespoons *each* **dry mint leaves** and **whole cloves,** and 1 tablespoon **dried lemon peel.**

ECCLEFECHAN RAISIN TART

Prepare this showy raisin-nut tart in a cake pan with a removable bottom; package it in a fancy box or tin for giving. Suggest serving the rich dessert in thin slices.

> **Butter Pastry (recipe follows)**
> 1 **egg**
> ½ cup firmly packed **brown sugar**
> ¼ cup **butter** or **margarine,** melted and cooled
> 1 tablespoon **wine vinegar**
> ½ cup *each* **dark raisins, golden raisins,** and chopped **walnuts**

Prepare Butter Pastry; press evenly over bottom and 1 inch up sides of an 8- or 9-inch cake pan with a removable bottom.

In a bowl, mix egg, sugar, butter, and vinegar until evenly blended. Stir in raisins and walnuts. Pour filling into pastry shell; spread to make level.

Bake on lowest rack in a 375° oven until firm in center when lightly touched (25 to 30 minutes). Let cool completely in pan on a rack.

Remove pan sides; then carefully lift tart from pan bottom, loosening with a knife if necessary. Transfer to a tin, gift box, or plate. Wrap airtight; store in refrigerator for up to 2 days. Makes 1 (8- or 9-inch) tart.

Butter Pastry. In a food processor or a bowl, combine 1 cup **all-purpose flour** and 2 tablespoons **granulated sugar.** Add ⅓ cup firm **butter** or margarine, cut into pieces; whirl (or rub with your fingers) until crumbly. Add 1 **egg yolk** to flour mixture and whirl (or stir with a fork) until dough holds together. With your hands, firmly press dough into a smooth ball. If made ahead, cover and refrigerate for up to 3 days; use at room temperature.

Lined with a traditional red and white checked tablecloth, then filled
with plain and spinach-flavored pasta (facing page), basil-scented Garden Marinara
Sauce (page 76), bread sticks, and a bottle of red wine, this Italian
dinner basket is ready to present as a novel gift.

ITALIAN PASTA DINNER BASKET

(Pictured on facing page)

Surprise special friends with a delightful basket loaded with everything they need for a cozy Italian dinner: a jar of homemade Garden Marinara Sauce, fresh plain and spinach-flavored pastas, bread sticks, and a bottle of red wine. If you like, you can also include a jar of Caponata or Peperonata for an appetizer. Arrange the meal-makings in a basket lined with a checked tablecloth and/or napkins; tie with a big bow. (Wrap the pasta airtight in plastic bags, plastic wrap, or cellophane.)

♥

Caponata or Peperonata (page 78)
Party Bread Sticks (page 22) or Purchased Bread Sticks
Homemade Pasta and/or Spinach Pasta (recipes follow)
Garden Marinara Sauce (page 76)
Red Wine

♥

HOMEMADE PASTA

Making perfect fresh pasta takes patience, but once you get the knack, the process moves smoothly, especially if you use a food processor to knead the dough and a pasta machine to roll and cut it.

Our basic recipe makes an all-purpose plain pasta to cut into noodles of any width you like. For variation in color and flavor, make the spinach version. When giving fresh pasta, be sure to attach a tag with cooking directions.

About 2 cups all-purpose flour
2 **eggs**
Water

To machine-mix and knead dough, put 2 cups flour, eggs, and 3 tablespoons water in a food processor; whirl until dough forms a ball (at least 30 seconds). If dough feels sticky when pinched, add 2 tablespoons more flour; process until dough forms a ball again (at least 30 more seconds). If dough is crumbly, add up to 3 tablespoons more water, 1 teaspoon at a time, processing after each addition. Divide dough into quarters; cover with plastic wrap and let rest for at least 10 minutes.

To hand-mix and knead dough, mound 2 cups flour in a bowl or on a board; make a well in center and add eggs. Beat eggs lightly with a fork; add 2 tablespoons water. Stir with a fork, drawing flour in from the sides, and adding 1 to 4 more tablespoons water, until dough is well mixed (it will be stiff). Pat into a ball and knead on a lightly floured board until dough feels smooth (about 10 minutes); add flour as required to prevent sticking, using as little as possible.

Divide dough into quarters; cover with plastic wrap and let rest for at least 10 minutes.

To roll and cut with a pasta machine, set rollers on widest opening. Flatten and lightly flour 1 portion of dough; feed through rollers, then fold into thirds lengthwise. Roll repeatedly until dough feels smooth and supple—10 to 20 times. If dough gets sticky, brush with flour; shake off excess.

Run dough through half-closed rollers. Reduce roller space to about $1/16$- to $1/32$-inch opening or narrowest setting (depending on how thick you want pasta to be); run dough through again. If dough gets too long to handle easily, cut strip in half or into thirds. Lay rolled sheets in a single layer on wax paper on a flat surface. Let dry, uncovered, until dough has the feel and flexibility of soft leather (5 to 10 minutes; if dried too long, pasta will be too brittle to cut well). Turn dough over 2 or 3 times as it dries.

Feed sheets, 1 at a time, through cutting blades of pasta machine.

If you are making the pasta ahead, lay cut strands out straight in single layers on wax paper. Cover with wax paper; roll up, enclose in plastic bags, and seal airtight. Refrigerate for up to 2 days or freeze for up to 2 months.

To roll and cut by hand, roll 1 portion of dough at a time on a lightly floured board until as thin as possible ($1/16$ to $1/32$ inch thick). Use as little flour as possible. Let dough dry as directed for machine-rolled pasta. When dry, cut into $1/4$-inch (or narrower) strips with a sharp knife (use a ruler as a guide) or noodle cutter.

Store as directed for machine-rolled pasta.

To cook pasta, in a 6- to 8-quart pan, bring 4 to 6 quarts water to a boil over high heat. Drop in 1 recipe Homemade Pasta (do not thaw, if frozen) and stir with a fork. Cook, uncovered, until just tender to bite (1 to 3 minutes). Drain well. Makes about 4 cups.

SPINACH PASTA. Cook $1/2$ package (10-oz. size) **frozen chopped spinach** according to package directions. Let cool, then squeeze out as much liquid as possible. Mince spinach finely; you should have $1/4$ cup. Then follow directions for **Homemade Pasta,** but add minced spinach with eggs and omit water.

Cook fresh Spinach Pasta for 2 to 3 minutes.

CLASSIC PICNIC HAMPER

(Pictured on page 95)

When sunny weather beckons, help get your friends' outings to beach or park off to a perfect start with a gift basket full of picnic foods and accessories. Our picnic spread features a robust homemade beef salami accompanied with dark pumpernickel or French bread, mustard, and pickles. For dessert, tuck in your choice of fresh fruits and cheese—and don't forget a bottle of wine.

To present the gift, line a woven hamper or basket with a picnic cloth or napkins; if desired, add pretty plastic plates and wine glasses, or a cutting board and knife.

Note: To make the salami, you'll need curing salt. It's available from butcher's equipment and supply companies and feed stores, or by mail order from some salt companies.

♥

Smoky Beef Salami (recipe follows)
**Molasses Pumpernickel Bread (page 21) or
French Bread**
Dijon-style Mustard (page 83)
Sweet Freezer Chips (page 81)
or
Spicy Seven-day Pickles (page 84)
Chunk of Sharp Cheddar or Swiss Cheese
Fresh Fruit of Your Choice
Wine

♥

SMOKY BEEF SALAMI

Make the original smoke-flavored version of this salami, or try the tasty variations.

    4   **pounds ground beef (maximum fat
        content about 25 percent)**
    ¼   **cup curing salt**
    2   **tablespoons liquid smoke**
    1½ **teaspoons garlic powder**
    1½ **teaspoons ground black pepper or 2
        teaspoons whole black peppercorns**

In a large bowl, *thoroughly* mix beef, salt, liquid smoke, garlic powder, and pepper. Cover and refrigerate for 24 hours.

Divide mixture into fourths. Shape each into a compact 8-inch log and place each on a 12- by 18-inch piece of nylon net (available at most fabric stores). Roll up tightly; tie ends with string. Place

logs on a broiler pan with a rack and bake in a 225° oven for 4 hours.

Remove salami logs from oven; remove net. Pat rolls well with paper towels to absorb excess fat. Let cool slightly, then wrap in foil and store in refrigerator for up to 3 weeks. To give, rewrap in cellophane or plastic wrap and tie ends with string or ribbon. Makes 4 logs of salami (about 3 lbs. *total*).

HERB BEEF SALAMI. Follow directions for **Smoky Beef Salami,** but make these changes. Omit liquid smoke and add 3 tablespoons **dry red wine.** Reduce garlic powder to 1 teaspoon and omit pepper. Instead, add 2 tablespoons **mustard seeds,** 1 tablespoon *each* **dry basil and dry oregano leaves,** 1 teaspoon **onion powder,** and ⅔ cup grated **Parmesan cheese.**

SPICY BEEF SALAMI. Follow directions for **Smoky Beef Salami,** but make these changes. Omit liquid smoke and add 3 tablespoons **dry white wine.** Reduce garlic powder to 1 teaspoon and omit pepper. Instead, add 2 tablespoons **chili powder,** 2 teaspoons **crushed red pepper,** and 1 teaspoon **ground cumin.**

FIRESIDE DESSERT BASKET

For frosty winter evenings, create this warming Scandinavian dessert buffet for eight. It would be especially welcome after a round of Christmas caroling or a day on the ski slopes.

Our Scandinavian Spiced Wine Kit provides everything you need for traditional *glögg*. To go with the hot punch, include a few goodies with a northern European flavor, such as Mazarin—little almond paste tarts—and Swedish Ginger Thins. Add crunchy glazed nuts and assorted fruits, and the basket is complete.

To present your gift, package the nuts and baked goods in an assortment of tins and boxes, then group them all in a Scandinavian red basket and wrap the whole package in cellophane; top with a bow or wooden Christmas ornaments.

♥

Scandinavian Spiced Wine Kit (facing page)
Mazarin (facing page)
Swedish Ginger Thins (facing page)
Penuche Pecans (page 11)
Assorted Dried and Fresh Fruits

♥

Scandinavian Spiced Wine Kit

  Spice Mix (recipe follows)
1 small orange
1 bottle (750 ml.) dry red wine, such as
  Burgundy, Zinfandel, or Gamay
½ cup whole blanched almonds

Prepare Spice Mix as directed; arrange in a gift box or tin along with orange, wine, and almonds.

On gift tag, include these preparation instructions. Pour Spice Mix into a 2-quart pan. Cut peel (colored part only, not white membrane) from orange in a long, thin strip; squeeze juice from orange. Add orange peel, orange juice, and wine to Spice Mix. Set over medium heat; stir occasionally until hot but not boiling. Add a few whole almonds to each serving. Makes 8 servings.

Spice Mix. In a cup or jar, layer ½ cup **sugar,** ½ cup **raisins,** 2 teaspoons **whole cloves,** and 2 **cinnamon sticks** (*each* 2 to 3 inches long). Cover tightly.

Mazarin

These simple but rich little tarts are a popular coffeetime snack in Scandinavia.

  Mazarin Pastry (recipe follows)
1 can or package (8 oz.) almond paste
2 tablespoons *each* granulated sugar and
  all-purpose flour
2 eggs
1 egg white
¼ teaspoon almond extract
1 cup powdered sugar
2 tablespoons milk

Prepare pastry and divide into 8 equal portions. Press each portion evenly over bottom and sides of a ½-cup plain or fluted tart pan. Set tart pans on a baking sheet.

Crumble almond paste into large bowl of an electric mixer; add granulated sugar and flour and stir to blend. Add eggs and beat until smooth; beat in egg white. Stir in almond extract.

Spoon an equal portion of filling into each pastry shell. Bake in a 325° oven until tarts are richly browned on top (about 35 minutes).

Let tarts cool in pans on a rack for about 5 minutes. Blend powdered sugar smoothly with milk; spoon evenly onto tarts, then spread to coat tops evenly. Let cool completely. Ease tarts from pans, using a knife tip to loosen. Wrap airtight; store at

room temperature for up to 2 days, in freezer for up to 1 month. Makes 8 tarts.

Mazarin Pastry. Stir together 5 tablespoons **sugar** and 1½ cups **all-purpose flour.** Rub in ½ cup (¼ lb.) firm **butter** or margarine (cut into small pieces) until evenly blended. With a fork, stir in 1 **egg yolk,** then press mixture with your hands to form a smooth ball. If made ahead, cover and refrigerate until ready to use; use at room temperature.

Swedish Ginger Thins

Though traditionally served at Christmas, these spicy cookies can be cut in many shapes to suit different occasions. Decorate the cookies with icing, if desired.

⅔ cup butter or margarine
⅓ cup *each* granulated sugar and firmly
  packed brown sugar
2 tablespoons dark corn syrup
2 teaspoons *each* ground ginger and cloves
1 tablespoon ground cinnamon
2 teaspoons baking soda
¼ cup water
2½ cups all-purpose flour
  Royal Icing (page 51), optional

In a medium-size pan, combine butter, granulated sugar, brown sugar, and corn syrup; place over medium heat and stir until butter is melted. Remove from heat, stir in ginger, cloves, and cinnamon, and let cool slightly. Stir baking soda into water and add to butter mixture, blending thoroughly. Then stir in flour until well combined (dough will be quite soft). Cover tightly with plastic wrap and refrigerate until firm (2 to 3 hours) or for up to 3 days.

On a floured board, roll out dough, a portion at a time, to a thickness of about ⅛ inch. Cut out with cookie cutters (about 2½ inches in diameter). If necessary, dip cutters in flour to prevent dough from sticking to them. Place cookies slightly apart on ungreased baking sheets. Bake in a 325° oven until slightly darker brown and firm to the touch (10 to 12 minutes). Transfer to racks and let cool completely.

If desired, prepare Royal Icing and press through a decorating tube, making swirls or other designs on cookies. Let icing dry; wrap cookies airtight and store at room temperature for up to 3 days, in freezer for up to 2 months. Makes about 5 dozen cookies.

Index ♥ ♥ ♥

This portable outdoor feast is sure to please any adventurous friend
who enjoys dining at the beach, in the park, or at a roadside table in the country.
Homemade Smoky Beef Salami (page 92) is accompanied with French
bread, cheese, fruit, Dijon-style Mustard (page 83), and wine.

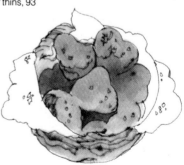

HOMEMADE

FROM THE KITCHEN OF

HOMEMADE

FROM THE KITCHEN OF

HOMEMADE

FROM THE KITCHEN OF

HOMEMADE

FROM THE KITCHEN OF

HOMEMADE

FROM THE KITCHEN OF

HOMEMADE

FROM THE KITCHEN OF

HOMEMADE

FROM THE KITCHEN OF

HOMEMADE

FROM THE KITCHEN OF

HOMEMADE

FROM THE KITCHEN OF

HOMEMADE

FROM THE KITCHEN OF

HOMEMADE

FROM THE KITCHEN OF

HOMEMADE

FROM THE KITCHEN OF

HOMEMADE

FROM THE KITCHEN OF

HOMEMADE

FROM THE KITCHEN OF

HOMEMADE

FROM THE KITCHEN OF

HOMEMADE

FROM THE KITCHEN OF

HOMEMADE

FROM THE KITCHEN OF

HOMEMADE

FROM THE KITCHEN OF

To order 3 additional sheets of labels, send a check or money order for $3.00 to:
Sunset Books, Gift Label Offer, 80 Willow Road, Menlo Park, CA 94025-3691